Nice Women
Get Divorced

The Conflicts and Challenges
for Traditional Women

Geneva Sugarbaker, M.S.

DEACONESS PRESS
Minneapolis, Minnesota

ISBN 0-925190-59-4
Library of Congress Catalog Card Number 92-072160

First Printing: October, 1992

Printed in the United States of America
96 95 94 93 92   7 6 5 4 3 2 1

Cover design by Michael Smith

Publisher's Note: Deaconess Press publishes books and pamphlets related to the subjects of physical health, mental health, and chemical dependency. Its publications, including *Nice Women Get Divorced*, do not necessarily reflect the philosophy of Fairview or Fairview Deaconess, or their treatment programs.

To Liz and Chris, for their love and encouragement

Acknowledgments

I would like to thank all of the women who so willingly and honestly shared their stories; they made the writing of this book possible. Even though few of these women knew each other, they became a kind of support group of "nice women" in my own journey towards autonomy. In reading this book, I hope you will experience the same kind of support from them that I have.

I would also like to thank my sisters and my parents, who enthusiastically supported the writing of this book even though divorce was a painful topic for all of us.

Special thanks to Florence Gifford, George Larson, Paul Johnson, and Jan Embretson, who were always there for me when I needed someone to listen or provide words of encouragement.

Finally, I want to thank my editor, Jack Caravela, who through his patience and expertise helped me realize my dream of publishing *Nice Women Get Divorced.*

Table of Contents

Preface

From my very first workshops which began in 1985, through the numerous interviews I've conducted with traditional women facing divorce, to the completion of this book, I have received input from several hundred women. During this process, some very strong common threads wove their way throughout.

The first thread that emerged as I spoke to women about the breakup of their marriages was the fact that they shared similar expectations regarding marriage and family. They all believed that they would get married, have children, and stay together as a family. Divorce was simply not an option.

The second thread was that almost all divorced women— whether they attended my workshops, were in a counseling setting, or were friends, acquaintances, or even strangers— expressed a vague sense of shame and guilt regarding their divorces. As a result, many of them viewed their divorces, and subsequently themselves, as failures. Some women admitted that they rarely told anyone, even family members, of the painful feelings they still carried with them.

A third thread that ran through both my own experiences and my research in writing this book was the fact that all women—regardless of race, socioeconomic background, or educational level—expressed similar conflicts and challenges surrounding divorce, their lost dreams, and their reduced financial status. It did not matter if they were experiencing the effects of a first or second divorce; their frustrations were universal.

The final thing that struck me time and time again was that even though most divorced women expressed a desire to improve the quality of their lives, they didn't know how to go about actually doing it. They spoke of feeling stuck and overwhelmed. Many of the women were struggling financially and felt victimized by their divorce. Some of them were still looking for Mr. Right to come along and rescue them.

This book is not just my story, but the stories of all of these women who have shared their lives and their pain. They are the ones who kept me motivated when the completion of this book seemed an overwhelming task.

Nice Women Get Divorced is a book for women who want to grow and who are willing to take an honest look themselves in order to do so. It is for women who want to become more capable, competent, and independent, to feel good about themselves and their lives, regardless of whether they remain single or remarry. In short, it is a book for and about all *Nice Women* who have struggled to keep their marriages and/or their families together and now face a life which is very different from the one they anticipated.

Introduction

The seed for *Nice Women Get Divorced* was planted in 1979 while I was living in a small rural community on the fringes of the Chicago suburbs. My second husband and I had bought a small, traditional nursery school which would become a thriving Montessori school in this somewhat provincial community.

The young mothers who brought their children to the school were pleased to have them exposed to such a positive learning environment, although they were a bit skeptical of the name "Montessori" and what it meant for their children. In time, however, they grew to trust me and my staff, and became quite enthusiastic as they saw a positive attitude towards learning developing in their young children.

In the late fall of that first year, one of the mothers was chatting with me at dismissal time and casually asked me if I had children of my own. "Oh yes," I answered proudly, "My daughter is in the third grade at Dean Street Elementary."

"Really?" she replied. "I'm a volunteer in the third grade there and I know all the children in the class. What's her name?"

"Liz," I answered proudly. "She's tall with blonde braids...very inquisitive. You would remember her."

"Liz...Liz Stephenson..." She was a bit puzzled, obviously trying to put the name with a face.

"Oh, no!" I laughed. "Liz Solliday! Her last name is different than mine."

She could not hide the shock and embarrassment on her face. She actually began to stammer and turn red. "I'm so sorry, Geneva," she said. It just didn't occur to me that you've been...*divorced*. You're so *nice!*"

I laughed and assured her that the confusion was understandable, and that she needn't feel embarrassed. With that she and her daughter were out the door, and I resumed dismissing the other children.

It wasn't until later that day as I was driving home from the school that the incident came back to me. I felt a surge of anger as I recalled her words: "You're so *nice*." I so clearly remember responding aloud as I drove through the streets of this sleepy rural town, "Yes, dammit, *nice women get divorced!*"

It wasn't until 1983, when I was confronted with the possibility that my second marriage might end, that I vividly recalled the incident at the Montessori school. It touched something within me—a deep gnawing pain that was difficult to put into words. I wondered if other "nice" women who were facing the possibility of divorce were feeling it, too. I began to read and study all that I could about the attitudes and socialization process which have affected us as women. How and why did we get where we are? What roles were we prepared for, and what roles were out of the realm of acceptable feminine behavior? Why was I struggling so? After all, I was capable and competent and, yes, so very *nice*. I was the traditional American wife and mother!

I began a Master's program in 1984 in Counseling and continued to explore the journey of women's lives. In 1985 I began conducting workshops for women facing divorce in conjunction with my Master's thesis. I titled them *Nice Women Get Divorced: Traditional Women Facing Divorce.* The response was emphatically positive. I utilized a model of personality development originated by psychologist Eric Berne to help women understand the origins of their emotions and why divorce—particularly for "nice" traditional women—is so difficult. Berne's model of Structural Analysis emerged as an effective tool for sorting out the plethora of ambivalent feelings that surround divorce.

Group counseling sessions grew out of the workshops, and the response was again positive and enthusiastic. The *Nice Women Get Divorced* sessions touched the lives of many women. As one participant put it, "The title caught my eye...I felt you were speaking to me. I feel I am a good person—a Nice Woman, and I wanted to hear what you had to say."

Since those early workshops, I have met many Nice Women whose traditional upbringings and values have been the source of great inner conflict when they found themselves facing divorce. This book is for all of the Nice Women I haven't met, but who are reading these words. Congratulations on taking the first step towards a better understanding of why we are the way we are, and changing your life for the better.

One

My Own Story:
Portrait of a Nice Woman

My own traditional roots are in Missouri, where I was born in 1946. Jefferson City is a river town—politically conservative, with a colorful history that speaks of the Civil War, riverboats, and American Indian lore.

I grew up at Orchard Acres, a place filled with more varieties of apple trees than I can recall. When I close my eyes I can still smell the fragrance of the orchard in bloom and hear the bees that collected pollen from the sweet blossoms every spring. It is easy for me to remember it as an idyllic life of long lazy summers playing on the bluffs of the Missouri River, or whiling away entire afternoons perched in an apple or sycamore tree just listening, thinking, or dreaming.

Like many other Nice Women, family played a very important role in my upbringing. There were ten young Sugarbakers growing up at Orchard Acres—four boys and six girls. I was the second oldest girl, which put me in a position of great responsibility. Most of the chores, such as cooking, cleaning, and laundry, fell on the shoulders of myself and my sisters. My father's philosophy was that "With six girls we don't need a maid." We learned the meaning of hard work, and grumbled that the Dutch must have originated the work ethic. We tolerated the frustration of the seemingly endless mounds of laundry and mismatched socks. We peeled pounds of potatoes and cored and sliced bushels of apples.

We worked in the orchard as well. Every summer my brothers ran an apple business and it was our job to help pick, sort, and polish the bushels of apples to be sold. On occasion, my brother would roust us out of bed in the early morning to help fill an order for a special customer. We strapped on the apple pickers (large canvas bags loaded with buckles and belts) like young ponies being harnessed for a race. We scurried to the tops of the trees where the best apples were in order to fill these cumbersome contraptions with the choicest selection.

Religion and church were also a big part of my upbringing, as they were for so many of the Nice Women who contributed their stories to this book. Our family attended a Southern Baptist church no less than twice a week. Every Sunday morning twelve Sugarbakers arrived, often late, to take their place in a pew at the front of the church. We were a colorful parade of ruffled dresses, patent leather pumps, and bonnets that were slightly askew. My brothers sported bow ties and white buck shoes. My mother was known for her wide brimmed straw hats. My father, tall and stately, led the processional.

I was baptized at that church on a cold gray Easter morning. A rather frail looking lady with cold hands and blue hair helped me into the choir gown in which I was baptized. I recall a kind of odd exhilaration as I was plunged into the warm baptismal in the name of "the Father, the Son, and the Holy Ghost."

For Sunday dinner my sisters and I helped our mother prepare four Southern fried chickens, mashed potatoes and gravy, biscuits, green beans, creamed corn and apple pie. When all the Sugarbakers sat down at the table, dinner became an event. My father always began the meal with a prayer. (He was deeply religious; his parents had raised him in the Dutch Reformed Church, and his faith was the cornerstone of our family.) Sometimes my sisters and I would nudge each other under the table when one of his prayers got especially long. Often we had the urge to giggle, but such disrespect would not have been tolerated.

My mother was also the child of Dutch parents. She was raised with the same type of Old World family values as my father's family. Her faith, too, was a source of family strength, and she has passed it on to all of her children.

When I was young, our summer vacations were spent on the shores of Lake Michigan. We would rent a cottage next to one occupied by our cousins, and my brothers and sisters and I would spend what seemed like endless days sliding down the dunes or playing hide and seek among the young saplings that grew profusely in the sandy terrain.

Some of my most vivid memories of growing up at Orchard Acres revolve around our holiday celebrations and the traditions that accompanied them. Christmas was a deeply religious celebration as well as a secular one in our family. It began with decorating the house inside and out. A large glass star was positioned at the highest point of our Christmas tree—a slightly tarnished reminder of the star of Bethlehem. As for our gifts on Christmas morning, dolls were usually the order of the day. Baby dolls, dolls that wet, dolls that talked, dolls and more dolls. With six girls, there were lots of them. I was more interested in horses and fringed jackets, but I always got a doll anyway. That was just what Santa Claus brought to little girls. Easter was another important day for our family. It was preceded by our dyeing dozens of eggs and hiding them for hours.

Easter Sunday itself started with church. We were dressed in our newest finery from head to foot. New hats, new shoes, new dresses, new ruffled socks and panties; we were our very own Easter parade, the perfect image of what little girls were supposed to look like.

My formal education, which began in 1951, was certainly a traditional one.   I attended public schools, because the only private ones were Catholic or Lutheran. If you lived on the west side of town, your school was all white, as mine was. The black families lived on the east side of town, and during my elementary years I never attended school with a student of another race.

For the time, I was considered a tomboy.   Much to my mother's chagrin, as I got older I insisted on wearing jeans to school. There were just three of us in my class, Carol, Phyllis, and I, who were "radical" enough to wear jeans and cowgirl boots on class picture day.   Seated in the front row of Miss Nellie's fourth grade class, we were a stark contrast to the skirts, anklets, and mary janes that the other girls wore.

Junior high brought the usual traumas—the ones that many girls still face. I was five feet eight inches tall, the same height I am now, and the boys were all about five-three. There were only two in my class that were as tall as me, and I didn't find either of them very appealing. It mattered a lot to me in those days that the object of my affection was only five-foot-two.

There were sock hops in the gymnasium, usually in the fall and spring. The girls generally loved these events because they were a legitimate excuse to get close to a boy, especially when Johnny Mathis was crooning "Smoke Gets in Your Eyes." I wasn't supposed to dance; it was against my parents' religion. But all of my friends went to the dances, so I begged and pleaded with my parents to let me go. They finally consented, with the agreement that I wouldn't actually dance! I remember sitting on the bleachers watching my friends do the twist to the rhythm of Chubby Checker. I felt painfully left out of the the fun they were obviously having.   Then, when I could stand it no longer, I decided to cope with the guilt and dance anyway. With a sudden burst of courage, I found the tallest boy I could and asked him to dance with me. It did not take long for my peers to notice that Geneva Sugarbaker was dancing! In fact, they cheered and clapped at my brave display of independence.

The next morning I decided to confess to my mother what I had done. (I was sure she would find out anyway from one of the girls in her Sunday School class.) She expressed extreme disappointment with my "worldly" behavior, but I can honestly say that although I appeared dutifully guilty, I was only a little bit sorry.

Eventually I settled on a tall boy who was to become my high school sweetheart. Rob was the love of my life, and my existence revolved around him. He became part of the family, and at times I thought he was more interested in playing with my younger brothers and sisters than he was in me.

Although Rob got along very well with my family, however, our relationship was far from smooth. We broke up and got back together more than any other couple I can remember. Still we managed to keep it going through our senior year. He was a star player for the Jeff City Jays—a football team in the midst of a record winning streak. Football was the school obsession. I was a pep squad member, and we followed the team to every game. As "Jayettes," we were perfectly happy to cheer for the boys. In those days, it never occurred to us to participate in a sport of our own.

The biggest honor a girl could have in high school was to be voted Homecoming Queen during her senior year. In keeping with its status in the school, it was the football team that nomimated the finalists. I can vividly recall the thrill I felt when my name was on the list. Then the final vote was put before the student body. I prayed that I would win, though I really didn't think I had a chance. The queen was usually a cheerleader— five-foot-two, blond, and well endowed.

I can still remember how happy I was when when I won. It was every girl's dream to be homecoming queen, to ride in a convertible in the homecoming parade, and to be crowned at halftime by her boyfriend, who was the captain of the football team.

After graduation, Rob and I went to different colleges for a year. I attended a small Baptist college while he went to the state university to play football. We continued to date off and on, and though our romance continued to be bittersweet, I remained loyal to him. I transferred to his school the next year, much to the disappointment of my parents. The university was much too worldly a place for them, but I wanted be near Rob.

At the end of our sophomore year, however, my world fell apart. Rob's grades weren't good, and he was placed on scholastic probation. The Vietnam War was raging, and Uncle Sam was looking for young, healthy football players who couldn't make the grade in college. Rob's choices were to enlist or get drafted. He joined the Marines, and our safe, innocent world would never be the same.

Within six months he got his orders for Vietnam. We were both scared and confused. Still, the news drew us closer together. We felt pressure to do something, to declare our love in a tangible way, a way that would somehow ease the pain of separation. We became officially engaged, much to the delight of our families. It was as if they too needed a balm to soothe their anxieties. The ring was white gold and bore a small diamond, but it felt like a foreign object on my hand. Looking back, I can honestly say we had no idea what we were doing.

He wrote to me from Vietnam, and I sent care packages. It took weeks for a box of cookies to make it to the DMZ, but I sent them anyway. I wrote to him every day and scoured the papers in dread of finding his picture among those of the casualities. Every time I received a long distance call, I was afraid it would be his parents, calling with tragic news. I used to wonder what I would do if he was killed.

Once I was sure I saw his picture in the Kansas City Star. It was of a wounded marine, and to me, the hazy black and white photo looked just like him. I drove from school to Jefferson City in a frenzy to see if his parents had seen the picture, or if they had heard from Rob. It turned out not to be him, but I'll never forget the cloud of helplessness and fear that hung over me during those interminable months of searching the newspapers.

I lived alone during my senior year; my former roommate had gotten married during the summer. Once again I was nominated for Homecoming Queen. This time, instead of the football team, my dormmates nominated me. Every women's dorm and each sorority nominated one person. After a series of interviews, seven women were left, including me. I was the only non-sorority candidate among the finalists.

Then, weeks before the election on campus, I got the news. My fiance had been wounded, shot in the back, and was recuperating in a hospital in DaNang. The bullet had just missed his spinal cord, and he was expected to recover. As soon as his schrapnel wounds were sufficiently healed, he would be flown to Hawaii for "R and R." He wanted me to meet him there. There was no question, of course, that I would go.

His parents sent me airline tickets with open dates, so that I would be able to go as soon as we received word that he was on his way to Honolulu. The day it came was the day before the election for Homecoming Queen. By noon of the following day, while the voting was going on at the campus voting booths, I was on my way from St. Louis to Honolulu to see my wounded fiance. Contrary to the feeling I had had four years before, the whole idea of running for Homecoming Queen suddenly seemed shallow. While my world on campus included taking classes, studying for exams, and now running for Homecoming Queen, his world had been one death and destruction in the jungles of Vietnam.

Our reunion was strained and awkward. It had been a year and a half of letters, loneliness, and the numbing of our fearful feelings. We were strangers—scared strangers in a tropical paradise. Neither of us knew what to expect of each other, but we had both changed. His boyish good looks had been replaced by a much older face. He had been through so much, and though I tried to understand, I couldn't begin to comprehend what he had experienced.

I was elected Homecoming Queen in absentia. When it was learned why the newly elected Homecoming Queen wasn't on campus to recieve the honor, there was quite a stir. The campus newspaper, as well as the Kansas City and St. Louis newspapers, lapped up this kind of story. The headlines read, "Queen Geneva in Hawaii Nursing Wounded Marine Fiance." I was something of a celebrity overnight. (Interestingly, the reporter for the college newspaper was Linda Bloodworth, now Linda Bloodworth-Thomason. She went on to create the television series *Designing Women*, populating it with characters who bear a striking resemblance to me and my sisters.)

Rob and I never married. I broke our engagement six weeks after he returned from Vietnam. I didn't know him anymore; he was very different from the naive young man to whom I had said goodbye two years before. It was the end of an era for me; my expectation of marrying my high school sweetheart had been shattered.

During the months and years that followed, I continued to live my life by trying to fulfill the traditional expectations that consciously or unconsciously influenced me. Upon my graduation from the university, I married someone I had known for a relatively short time. Like many Nice Women, I married right out of school. Living independently and on my own was not an option; it simply didn't fit my expectation of getting married and having a family. Not until my second marriage began to crumble some fifteen years later did I begin to examine my life—past and present—in order to understand what my traditional upbringing had meant to me; how it had influenced my choices, and consequently my struggles.

What I have discovered during these past five or six years is that my traditional past is not just a collage of random memories, but rather a tightly woven tapestry that *is* me. That tapestry includes my parents, who are still married and who still live in the house where I grew up. It includes the holidays and vacations spent with my brothers and sisters: Thanksgivings gathered around the dinner table, Christmas Eves at candlelight church services. It includes high school sweethearts, engagement dinners, and dreams of the perfect marriage. It includes expectations of my own happy, smiling children celebrating birthdays with mom and dad standing by with the camera. Finally, it includes a desire for security and stability—my own kids growing up in the same white house on the hill where I spent my childhood, with the same certainty that no matter what, the family would stay together.

I never envisioned a broken marriage, single parenting, transitional housing, or financial worries as part of my life. No late support payments, weekend visitations, or split holiday celebrations. These are not part of my tapestry, and they do not fit into the pasts of the many divorced women with whom I have come in contact. Even though divorce is a fact of life, it was not supposed to be a fact of *our* lives.

For Nice Women, myself included, divorce was never an option. We were committed to our marriages just as our parents were, and we planned to stay married, raise our families, and celebrate our fiftieth wedding anniversaries with our grandchildren. For this reason, many of us stayed in our marriages long after we should have let go. We stayed for the many reasons which we will examine in the next chapter.

Before going on, you may want to take some time to complete the following exercise. It asks you to reflect on your own past, recalling those childhood memories and perceptions that you still carry with you. It encourages you to think of your growing-up years as a large family album full of pictures from your own unique past. Throughout this book we will be drawing on these pictures, reexamining them in new lights.

EXERCISES FOR SELF-DISCOVERY

Reexamining the Pictures in Our Family Albums

Imagine your own personal picture album from your past. Each picture depicts a significant event that has influenced you and the expectations that you carry with you as an adult.

What pictures do you recall when your think of marriage, family, and security?

What pictures come to mind as you think back on holidays, vacations, and celebrations, such as birthdays and anniversaries?

Now that you have formed the mental pictures of your album, consider the following questions:

In what way does the reality of your current life differ from the pictures in your album, and from your expectations?

Which pictures cause you to experience the greatest pain and/ or conflict as you try to come to terms with your life today?

Two

Why We Stay

When it comes to marriage and family, Nice Women share common values and expectations. After all, we were raised on Donna Reed and June Cleaver. We never questioned that someday we would have a husband, run a household, and raise our children. This was the case with Kathryn McCoy, a woman I met at one of my workshops.

Kathryn grew up in a small Iowa town, the oldest of four children in a traditional American family. Her father was Vice President of the local bank, and her mother took care of the home and family. Kathryn was an "A" student, a cheerleader, and secretary of her high school class of '72. After graduation she attended Iowa State University, where she planned to major in Elementary Education. It was during her freshman year that she met and fell in love with Thomas McCoy, a dashing prelaw student who became the focus of her life.

Fifteen months later they were married. The couple had a lovely traditional church wedding in Kathryn's hometown. Tom, of course, continued with his pursuit of a law degree. Kathryn put her college plans on hold temporarily, until Tom could begin his practice and support them both.

A year after their wedding, Thomas Jr. was born. Kathryn was a good mother and a supportive wife. Somehow she was able to juggle her job on campus, caring for her son, and the emotional support of her husband, whose law school schedule demanded long and grueling hours of study.

Eventually her husband began practicing law, but by this time Emily was born, and Joshua was on the way. Kathryn's days were full and her nights were long, and for now, returning to school to finish her degree just wasn't practical.

Fifteen years later, never having found the time to return to school, Kathryn McCoy's small secure world came apart, and she found herself divorced, a single parent of four children with no career. This was something Kathryn never anticipated. "I expected to be married for the rest of my life to a successful husband," she told me, "with all the good traditional things my mother had."

Now at thirty-nine, working and attending college at night, struggling to meet the demands of four teenagers, she faces a whole new life—a life for which she was not prepared.

The women for and about whom this book is written are women like Kathryn McCoy. Women for whom divorce is the last option, Nice Women raised in traditional homes by traditional parents, who had traditional expectations placed upon them as little girls.

The experiences of Nice Women affected by divorce are marked by certain patterns that emerge in their lives, revealing stong similarities in their values and expectations regarding marriage and family. Over and over again, as Nice Women have shared their hopes, wishes and dreams with me about marriage and family, ten common characteristics have emerged. They reveal a great deal about us and our socialization process. By examining them, we can begin to understand why divorce is the very last option to be considered, and why it has such a devastating impact on our lives.

1. Nice Women have often seen their parents endure long-lasting marriages, many reaching their fortieth or fiftieth wedding anniversaries.

When discussing divorce, Nice Women consistently make references to their parents' marriages, most of which have lasted many years. For many of us, the fact that our parents stuck it out "for better or worse" magnifies the loss when our own marriages end. Guilt and a sense of failure resulting from a comparison to parents' marriages are evident in the following responses from two Nice Women:

> "I've often asked myself why my parents were able to make it work when I couldn't. There is no doubt that I feel I've failed because I'll never achieve the landmark of a fiftieth wedding anniversary."

The expectation of maintaining a family history like her parents' emerges in this woman's story:

> "I vividly remember my parents' fiftieth wedding anniversary. My whole family was there, and we watched old family movies. Before me was my history as a child—vacations, birthday parties, Christmas, my first prom. There were my brothers and sisters and my parents, all sharing this same history. My husband and I had just reconciled for the second time, and I clung to the hope that we too would share our fiftieth anniversary. We were ultimately divorced three years later."

A feeling of being isolated and alone, without a family reference point, is another response that has been expressed by a number of Nice Women. This woman from Boston puts the feeling into words:

> "This characteristic is certainly true of me. My parents have been married over fifty years, so when I got divorced I had no reference point. It was like stepping out on the ice of a huge frozen lake. There were no roads. There was nothing in front of me but ice. I had no way of knowing how my life would change, or how to live my life as an unmarried woman."

While many of us admire the longevity of our parents' marriages, it is true that some women express negative memories of their parents' long and enduring relationships. This is to be expected; after all, we observed our parents go through difficult times. Some women recall a childhood yearning for something better:

> "As a teen I remember thinking that I didn't want a marriage like my parents'. My father was moody and domineering—very wrapped up in his work. My mother was in awe of him, and rarely confronted him on anything; we all walked on eggs in his presence. Once, after they had had a really big fight in which my father had treated my mother very badly, I said to her, 'You should divorce him.' She reeled in her anger and told me *never* to mention that word again."

Eve Tolley, a writer and psychotherapist from Connecticut who works with women, sums up this characteristic of being able to view our parents' marriages critically as one which only recently has become at all common. Her view is that women who have come of age in the late fifties, sixties, and seventies have a hard act to follow when it comes to our parents and their marriages.   One thing that was a primary feature in these marriages, according to Tolley, is that they *endured.*

Endurance may have been our parents' key to long marriages, and perhaps we are not willing to endure as much today. Nevertheless, Nice Women go to great lengths to try to salvage their marriages, and they deeply grieve their loss. Most admit they tried desperately to hold on to what they perceived that their parents have—long-lasting, traditional marriages. When asked if divorce occured to them in the early stages of dysfunction in their marriages, their answers are emphatic. One woman's response speaks for many:

> "No! Absolutely not! The lesson that I learned from my mother was that if you endure long enough and well enough, the marriage will last."

The reality for many of us is, of course, that our marriages do end.

2. Nice Women have grown up believing they would marry, have children, and live happily ever after.

Most of the Nice Women who have contributed to this book viewed getting married and having a family as an understood expectation of their childhood. It wasn't as much a conscious choice as an inherent right. Only spinster aunts and schoolmarms were single, and childless women were either pitied or viewed as selfish.

Leah, 39, now an associate professor and published writer, tells this story, which parallels the lives of many Nice Women:

> "This characteristic was certainly true for me to the extent that I wanted to do this more than go to college. As a high school graduate, I had no ambition—no ambition

at all. The word 'career' wasn't in my vocabulary. I was painting then, and I thought 'I'll get married and I'll paint.' But it was always within the context of marriage.

"I was traumatized about going away to college because it was a postponement of what I pictured my life to be—getting married and having children. Which is, of course, exactly what I did. I came home from my freshman year at college having flunked out because of poor grades. I married my high school sweetheart at nineteen and had a baby at twenty.

"The difficulty for me was that after you do those two things, what do you do next? At twenty, 'happily ever after' seemed like a long time."

Fantasies about marriage, of taking care of a husband and being taken care of, dominated the early lives of many Nice Women. Even upon graduating from college, we generally were not looking towards careers and independence. As I approached my graduation from the university, I wasn't even thinking about making a living. Even though I had broken my engagement a few months earlier, I was still trying to live out my dream. I had just seen the movie *A Man and a Woman* and I wanted to serve breakfast to my husband dressed in white satin pajamas just as Anouk Aimeé had done.

In order to fulfill my fantasy, I married a younger man I had known less than a year and had a baby nine and a half months later. The pregnancy terminated my teaching contract, so I began selling cosmetics six weeks after my daughter was born. I was supporting the three of us while my husband finished school. My fantasy ended quickly.

This early childhood belief in the "happily ever after" of marriage is not something that I, or other Nice Women, viewed as glib or silly. It was, and still is, a value that supports the traditional feminine self-concept. Consequently, when it is shattered, part of our self-concept is shattered also. Leah's experience illustrates this, as well as the guilt that accompanies the destruction of this part of our identities:

> "When I realized my marriage was failing, I felt guilty that I wasn't able to achieve this 'happily ever after' idea. I held on for a long, long time simply to try to preserve what I honestly believed was my *right*. Ultimately, I felt there was something wrong with me, that I had failed."

Numerous childhood messages supported this expectation of "happily ever after," from fairy tales to movies to television to the print media—women have always been a vulnerable target. Advertisers have always appealed to our romantic fantasies. A full page ad for a jewelry company featuring a dreamy-eyed blonde which appeared in *Look* magazine on March 9, 1971 encapsulates the traditional romantic fantasy. The copy reads: "The prince or cowboy or the somebody you never told anybody about when you were a child is suddenly real. And you're going to marry him. A diamond is forever." Diamonds, yes— marriages, not necessarily. But then, advertisers don't make money on divorce. Lawyers do.

3. As little girls, Nice Women fantasized about being taken care of emotionally and financially by their strong, protective husbands.

The reality of facing divorce, being alone, single parenting, and becoming financially self-sufficient is a far cry from this childhood expectation of protection, yet many women admit to having sincerely believed in it. A study on marriage conducted in the early 1970s revealed that many women viewed marriage as a fortress which would protect them from responsibility. Financial security was high on the list of what many women in this survey wanted from a husband. And why not? That's what many of our fathers had provided for our mothers. One woman, a bank president's daughter, puts it this way:

> "In my family, my father made the money and managed it. In fact, it wasn't even 'proper' to talk about money— it was just there. He gave my mother money each week, and she used it for groceries and incidentials. Any purchases had to be approved by him. Sometimes my sisters and I would charge new clothes and then hide them until my mother could find the 'right' time to tell him. He often complained about the clothing bills, but we never for a moment worried about them not getting paid."

In my own life, it wasn't until my second marriage was falling apart that I was forced to confront this expectation in myself. For the first time in my life I realized I was not going to be taken care of. I was forty years old, and the reality of having to support myself and my children was paralyzing. I had nightmares about bills piling up and not being able to pay them. I would wake up frozen with fear.

When responding to questions about financial responsibilities in a marriage, many Nice Women admitted to believing that male-provided security was actually their right. Hope, a forty-four year old teacher from Missouri, illustrates this in the following reflection:

> "I thought I would be taken care of financially. I actually thought that was one of those God-given rights, that I would marry a man and he would take care of me. I might contribute financially, but ultimately he would be the breadwinner and the manager of the money."

This concept that we would be taken care of has played a strong role in the lives of Nice Women, and like our other beliefs, it is blown apart by divorce. The no-fault divorce laws have resulted in fewer and fewer women receiving alimony or maintenance from an ex-spouse. At the same time, the cost of living and the need for more training and education for better paying jobs continues to escalate. When the financial reality of divorce and the fantasy of this traditional belief are juxtaposed, they simply cannot be reconciled.

4. Nice Women have seen friends, acquaintances, and sometimes siblings go through divorce, and secretly thought it would never happen to them.

Women whom I have interviewed or who have attended my workshops admit to having felt this way at some time or other prior to facing divorce themselves. Janice, now divorced and in her mid-forties, recalls having this attitude:

"I watched my neighbor in our rather affluent community go through her divorce. I watched her lose her house, her expensive car, and her status, and I felt a little smug about my own security. Ironically, the problems in my own marriage which ultimately resulted in my divorce existed back then. I just wasn't willing or able to see them."

This denial that another woman's situation could happen to us often applies within our families as well as to ourselves. Just as we feel that what has happened to another woman couldn't happen to us, we often feel that it can't or shouldn't happen to someone in our own family. Anna, a member of a large traditional family that had gained notoriety within its community, recalls how her sister's divorce affected her:

"I felt sorry for her, and yet at the same time, I was angry that she had marred our family's reputation. It was different when it happened to someone else's family, but I guess I felt we were 'above' divorce. It wasn't until I was going through my own divorce that I realized what she must have felt—an enormous sense of guilt for letting her family down."

This expectation that we will stay married often promotes the denial of real issues within our relationships, as if staying married was, in and of itself, a solution to dysfunction in a marriage. Rather than looking for ways to resolve the problems, many of us focused on "just staying married." Paula, now remarried at forty-two, recalls her adherence to this belief in her first marriage, as well as the futility of it:

"To tell you the truth, I stayed in my first marriage for eleven years, and yet that marriage was over in three. As I watched others getting divorced, I secretly wished I had the courage to do it, but I didn't. We kept regrouping just to keep the marriage together. It finally resulted in sort of a double standard—my real life versus the shell of my married life. It wasn't until my thirties that I could resolve this dilemma. My way of acting out this belief was to lead a 'double life.'"

"Leading a double life," "feeling falsely secure," and "being above divorce" are themes of denial that permeate the lives of traditional women in dysfunctional marriages. Our willingness to *pretend* that our marriages are intact, regardless of the personal compromises we often make in order to do so, illustrates the enormous impact that our early conditioning has on our attitudes toward marriage.

5. *Nice Women value keeping their families intact.*

Traditional families stay intact, and Nice Women fight to keep their families together. Though statistical trends support the fact that traditional nuclear families are on the decline, this does not make it easier for Nice Women to face the breakup of their families. Family unity is probably the one thing Nice Women work the hardest to maintain. An aversion to a "broken home" has been branded into our minds.

The breakup of my second marriage parallels the experiences of other Nice Women I have interviewed. The fact that it was my second marriage in many ways made the divorce more difficult, because we were already a *blended* family—his daughter and my daughter. In six years the girls had become very close and called each other "sister." Then we had our son—a brother to each of the girls, which I felt brought us closer together as a family. It was as if the pain of my first divorce had finally healed, and it was inconceivable to me that this new family that we had created would crumble. I stayed in the marriage seven or eight years after the trust was gone, primarily to keep our family intact.

The hardest thing for me to accept through my three year separation and ultimate divorce was that my son wouldn't grow up with his dad around. I wanted that for him more than anything. Years later, I'm still working to let go of that dream.

Of course, Nice Women without children often fight just as hard to keep their families together. Husbands and wives are families, and marriages create bonds between their relatives. Lorrie, who was divorced after thirteen years, shares her story, which is a common one:

"My mother-in-law and I had become very close. She was like the mother I never had. I also had inherited brother-in-laws and sister-in-laws and nieces and nephews. I didn't want to lose all of that. I wasn't just getting a divorce from my husband, I was losing other people as well."

This expectation of keeping our family together continues to be important to Nice Women even after divorce. Deb, who has been a single parent for several years, speaks for many of us as she tells of her struggle to hold on to this value:

"Even after my divorce, this continued to be an enormous priority for me: to *look* like a family if nothing else—at all costs. As a single mother, I know I have overcompensated for the fact that we aren't a traditional family. You can't do everything as a single parent, but I have tried, and in many ways, have been both a mother and father to my boys."

Families today take many shapes and forms. The terminology abounds—"blended families," "step-families," "single parent families," and yes, "traditional nuclear families." When Nice Women were growing up, however, *family* simply meant one thing: mom, dad, and the kids. If Nice Women had their way, they would keep their families *intact*.

6. Nice Women fight to save their marriages at all costs— believing that if they try hard enough, love enough, understand enough, forgive enough, and change enough, they can make their marriages work.

Nice Women are like chameleons. We change and adapt with relative ease, believing that we can alter circumstances because of our intuitive ability to read a situation and make the necessary adjustments. When I asked women to respond to this statement, all of them acknowledged that they had jumped through at least one, if not all of the following "hoops" in order to save their marriages:

Some Nice Women did all they could to shield their marriages from financial problems:

"Looking back, I can hardly believe all of the contortions I went through. During our twelve year marriage, I did everything humanly possible to keep our marriage going. I helped him when his business continually floundered; I worked out payment plans with the I.R.S. I answered the door when the sheriff delivered the summons for non-payment."

Some Nice Women catered to their husband's egos in an effort to keep their marriages going:

"I waited with special meals and dressed in sexy gowns when he came off the road. I believed in him. I told him he was handsome and wonderful. I dressed like he wanted me to dress."

Some Nice Women believed that they held the magic key to making their spouses happy, thus keeping their marriages intact:

"When he said he wasn't happy, I thought, 'I'll make you happy.' Each time we regrouped, I figured out a new plan of attack. Twice we went into counseling."

Some Nice Women thought self-improvement would counteract a spouse's affair and, consequently, save their marriages:

"Even after he blatantly began to carry on an affair, I took tennis lessons because *she* played tennis. Even then, I actually believed that I could figure a way to make our marriage work."

The effort to adapt to a husband's needs in order to keep the marriage together is characteristic of most Nice Women's experiences. It is a direct result of our traditional feminine socialization process, and most women confess to doing it automatically. Deb, who shared her single parenting struggle earlier, recounts her efforts to become more adaptable in her marriage:

> "This was always true of me—always the self-examination as the marriage started to fall apart. I always believed I was wrong. Even to this day, part of me believes I was wrong. I wasn't moldable. I was 'too this' or 'too that.' I couldn't change or adjust enough.
> "I tried being many different people...throwing myself into many different aspects of being a good wife. I was an Air Force wife for seven years of our twelve year marriage. Looking back, I realize there was nothing more antithetical to my nature. But I molded myself as best I could and walked my babies with the other Air Force wives."

Moving is another adjustment that Nice Women commonly make when their husbands' careers demand it. Many women recall uprooting their families' lives in order to accommodate a husband's promotion or job change, even though their marriage was floundering. For many of them it not only meant leaving a good job of their own, it also served to delay the breakup of their marriage:

> "I gave up an excellent teaching position in the early seventies that I was never able to replace because my field was so limited. I recall being very depressed about the move and leaving behind a program I had worked so

hard to create. But it never occured to me not to go.
Though I worked at a number of lesser jobs, I was never
able to replace my full-time teaching position in theatre,
or the financial self-sufficiency I had had. We divorced
five years later, but the writing had always been on the
wall."

"Adapting," "molding," "changing," "regrouping," and "fig-
uring out a new plan" are only a few of the ways Nice Women
describe the strategies they used to make their marriages work.
The reality is, of course, that these maneuvers do not resuscitate
a dying marriage.

7. *Nice Women rate highly the needs of their children and husband, usually putting them above their own.*

Nice little girls raised in traditional homes got the message
early. "Take care of others...respond to others...be sensitive to
the needs of others." Sometimes the message was loud and clear.
Sometimes it was subtle and manipulative, but regardless of how
it was sent, we got it. And the more we responded, the more we
were praised, and the more we were praised, the better we felt. So
it isn't surprising that nice little girls who grow up to be wives and
mothers continue to be caring, responsive, and sensitive to the
needs of others.

This theme runs throughout the stories of Nice Women.
Unfortunately, it often means forfeiting our own needs as we
attend to those of others. Or, if we do pursue needs of our own,
we feel pressured to make sure no one else is inconvenienced.
Eileen's experience with returning to school illustrates this
belief, and the feelings of guilt that often accompany it:

"Our marriage had been shaky for about three years
when I decided to go to back to school. I felt guilty about

making this choice, and made sure that my family experienced no inconvenience because I was studying or writing papers. I worked harder to keep up the laundry and the meals in order to compensate for my guilt."

Denying the value of one's own needs always has consequences, and these consequences usually "come out sideways" until they are addressed. Joan, who is still trying to work out the problems in her marriage, learned this when she sought professional help for chronic depression. Like many Nice Women, she did not link her symptoms with the fact that she continually denied her own needs:

"I'm getting better at not putting my family's needs above my own, but I still have a strong tendency to do it. It's as if I feel I am some wealth of resources and they—meaning my family—have limitations. It wasn't until I sought help for a period of intense depression that I was able to understand the fact that *always* denying my own needs in favor of those of my husband and children was actually contributing to my chronic depression."

Women have often told me of supressing their own needs over and over, as if by doing so they might finally make their marriages right. Beth, who recently ended a ten year second marriage, describes her experience playing out this role:

"I was working to support the family, yet all of the money I made went to support my husband's car racing hobby. For a struggling young couple this was a rather frivolous expense, though I rarely voiced disapproval or disagreement. I guess I truly felt it was important for him to maintain his hobby, while I supressed my own aspirations—career-wise and personally. I had seen my mother do this for my father."

Putting everyone else's needs first is common, but the real issue behind this behavior goes much deeper. The following story reveals a dramatic result of the sacrifices which are encouraged in a traditional feminine upbringing. Rae's experiences reveal how serious the effects of self-denial can be. She joined one of my counseling groups shortly after her twenty-two year marriage ended:

> "After my third child I gained weight, which just became impossible to lose. No matter what diet I tried or what exercise class I enrolled in, I always let it go to meet my family's immediate needs. Over and over this happened, and the more frustrated I got, the more I ate. I felt helpless to stop it. What I came to realize was that I truly didn't feel I deserved to make time for me. I just wasn't that important."

This theme of "not being important enough" consistently runs through the stories of Nice Women. It's as if in the process of meeting the needs of others, we forgot to develop a self of our own. Perhaps that's why "doing for others" simply feels not only more gratifying, but also more familiar.

8. Nice Women worry the most about how divorce will affect their children.

For Nice Women who are mothers, the effects of divorce on their children is the most critical and painful issue to be faced. At the beginning of a workshop or a group counseling session on divorce, I often ask the participants to write down the one question they would most like to have answered about divorce. Over and over again, the most asked questions are:

"How will divorce affect my children?"

"Will my children be hurt by the divorce?"

"How can I go ahead with something that I know will hurt my children?"

In one form or another, this is the burning issue. The depth of this dilemma is illustrated by Leah, the professor and writer we met earlier, in her rather grim analogy:

> "The problem is that you don't have any reference point. You really don't have any idea how the divorce is affecting your children. It reminds me of Anna Freud's study of the children of Auchwitz...displaced, orphaned. No one knew how those traumas would affect those children until much later, when years had passed and studies were done."

Anxiety and inner conflict are ever present when Nice Women try to sort out solutions which conflict with the values of an earlier generation. Because our parents "stuck it out for the sake of the children," it is much more difficult to break up the image of the traditional family, even if our children may be negatively affected by keeping the family intact. Elizabeth, who in her words "stayed too long in an abusive relationship," illustrates this conflict in the following account:

> "Oh, goodness, I have worried about this one. I was caught in a bind that I think many women are caught in. Is the father that my children have in an abusive relationship better than no father at all? The message that I had gotten from my parents and their generation was that any father—because of what he could provide

financially and in terms of an image of stability—was better than no father at all. I finally resolved this dilemma, but only with the help of a skilled therapist."

When asked to recall childhood friends from divorced homes, most Nice Women could recall no more than one or two. We all remember our parents referring to these children as being from "broken homes," as if they were different from us in some fundamental and negative way. Today, our own children have many friends whose parents are separated. Once again Leah provides her opinion of this situation:

"It is a relatively recent 'baby boom' phenomenon that there are so many stepchildren, stepfamilies, 'instant families,' single mothers, weekend dads, and so on. I don't think we really know yet what the effects will be on our children. I don't know if we will ever know the full effects. I think it is a terrible source of grief for them."

It is true that families today take on many forms, and that the number of nontraditional families is increasing. However, for Nice Women, this trend provides little comfort when it comes to *their* families and *their* children.

The worry list goes on and on. We worry about our children's social development as well as their school performance. And the more we worry, the more we conclude that is is best to keep the marriage together at all costs to ourselves. If we do divorce, we may scrutinize every situation and weigh it against the effects of divorce, as Gail did. Her story is typical of other Nice Women who are single parents:

"Every time my son cried or got his feelings hurt, I looked for reasons beyond the obvious. When his playmates called him a 'sissy,' I wondered if it would be

different if there were a man around. If he got in trouble
at school, or had a nightmare, or was sullen, I wondered
if he was angry about not being a family anymore. I
continually examine his behavior in light of the divorce."

Nice Women also worry about their children's abilities to
form lasting relationships. I know that I have this concern for my
daughter. Because her father and I separated when she was six,
I worry that this has affected her ability to form healthy relationships with men. While in college she sought counseling for what
she now terms her "abandonment issues" so that she could learn
to understand the painful feelings she kept reexperiencing in
close relationships.

Lois, a single mother of a teenager, shares a similar concern
for her son:

"I believe my nineteen year old has trouble committing
to an intimate relationship. We have talked about it. He
can do the sexual stuff, but he has trouble with intimacy—
with any feelings of vulnerability. He watched his father
and I go through so much, the end result of which was our
divorce. It was very painful for all of us."

Whatever the scenario or the specific issue, concern about
our children's well-being is a neverending battle within us.
Renee, who has been a single parent for five years, summarizes
the problem effectively:

"In my opinion, it is a much greater problem—or at least
as great a problem—for children to live in a family
where the parents simply aren't happy. Whether they
fight continually or keep it a secret from the family, there
are long-term scars from this, too. But if your love your
children and communicate this to them, and their father

communicates this, perhaps they are better off in a divorced situation."

Renee's perspective is most likely correct; sometimes children *are* better off in a divorced situation. However, this fact doesn't make it any easier for Nice Women to resolve their fears and concerns.

9. Nice Women are "Super Wives"—"Super Moms"—"Super Women."

This characteristic is closely related to ones we have already discussed. It becomes clear when we examine the lives of Nice Women—married or single, divorced or separated. The Super Woman Syndrome emerges as a common pattern.

Nice Women are typically involved in many activities which are related to their families, children's schools, churches, and communities. We can be seen at little league games, ballet recitals, and music lessons. We give great birthday parties and make clever Halloween costumes.

We teach Sunday School and sing in the church choir. We are room mothers, volunteers for the school fun fair, and help our children with their homework.

We entertain for our husbands and attend their business functions. We often help our husbands in their work. We may hold full or part-time jobs or go back to school. Somehow we manage to keep all of the balls in the air, often without expecting any help.

Eve Tolley, the psychotherapist from Connecticut whose ideas we've discussed, tells of her experience returning to school to get her graduate degree in Social Work:

"I have always been guilty of trying to be a 'Super Woman.' I recall the time when I was working on my

master's degree. My time to do my reading and writing
started after ten p.m.—after I had served a good dinner,
after I made sure my children's homework was done,
after their baths and bedtime stories were complete.

"When they were tucked in and the laundry was
done, then I would take time for myself. I would work
from ten p.m. until two or three o'clock in the morning,
and then I would be up early to get everyone off to school.
I would keep this up for three or four days, until the
weekend, when I would collapse. Nobody knew I was in
school but me."

Eve's story is typical of the way many Nice Women over-
compensate for meeting their own needs. Even when faced with
the possibility of divorce, with its accompanying strain and risk
of depression, Nice Women rarely slow down. In fact, we often
continue to function as if the impending divorce were not a
factor. Rather than taking care of ourselves, we continue to fool
ourselves into believing that our uninterrupted caretaking is
indispensible to those around us. Gail, who readily admitted to
succumbing to the Super Woman role, explained how this trait
affected her throughout her divorce:

"It didn't occur to me for a long time that I should slow
down and let a few things go. I pushed myself harder
than ever during the separation and divorce. I felt like a
taut rubber band. I couldn't admit I needed time just for
me, to relax, rest, and nurture myself. I felt like I was on
a treadmill—I became tense, distraught, and short-
tempered. I cried when things didn't meet my
expectations, but I just kept pushing."

This trait is deeply engrained, and is not easily modified,
even during divorce, when we are so prone to physical and

emotional exhaustion. Even when we realize that such overzealous caretaking isn't healthy, we still find it difficult to change. Corine's story expresses this well:

> "I was definitely a 'Super Woman' before my divorce, and for a long period afterward. I have since struggled to establish realistic expectations of myself. I try to say 'no' more, but I have to work at it. My automatic response is to slip back into the Super Woman mode. I will probably always have to be conscious of not overextending myself. I've always done it—it's my Achilles heel."

The fact that so many Nice Women admit to *always* having played the Super Woman role illustrates how powerful the traditional expectations that we have of ourselves really are, especially when it come to taking care of the needs of our families.

10. Nice Women gauge their own success by the success of their husband and/or children.

When we review the previous beliefs, values, and expectations, it is no surprise that Nice Women feel their husband's and children's success reflects their own. After all, we have put their needs first; we have nurtured and supported them. We have been Super Wives and Super Moms. If they win, we win. If they lose, we lose. This is our nature. The following comments from Nice Women reveal a variety of ways we have supported this belief in our behavior.

Assisting in a husband's career climb is a common theme. Sue, now forty-four, shares her story of playing this role in her early twenties, and later in her second marriage:

"As my husband was climbing the corporate ladder, I made great sacrifices to support him. He insisted that elaborate entertaining was essential to perpetuate the right business contacts. Any socializing we did was done to develop prospective clients, or to show clients how successful he was. I put a lot of time and energy into promoting his success, and yes, I did feel his success was my success."

Parental values also play a role in this belief. If our family of origin valued success, we learned to value it also. And since many of us were not oriented toward careers of our own, we often seek success through our mates. This phenomenon is common among women from traditional families. Sherry's story, which reflects the value placed on a husband's success, is typical of many Nice Women:

"I so much wanted my husband to be successful. I was from a highly professional family, and he wasn't. It didn't matter to me whether or not he was a doctor or a lawyer, but it did matter to me whether or not he was successful. If he failed, I failed. When his business floundered over and over again, I was angry at him for not being a 'success.' It took me a very long time to disengage from his failures, and to believe they were not a reflection on me. Looking back, this was a significant factor in our divorce."

Disenchantment with a mate's lack of success emerges as a frequent theme among traditional women, often contributing to the demise of the marriage. Additionally, Nice Women admit to being *emotionally* affected by a mate's choice of career, whether successful or not. It's as if we are experiencing our *own* careers vicariously through our husbands, as many of our mothers did.

Karina, who is now back in school in order to train for her own career, admitted to identifying emotionally with her first husband's career decisions:

> "Yes, I felt I was connected with his success, but I also had a lot of trouble with this because I didn't always agree with his choices. For example, when he quit being an airline pilot—which I thought was kind of romantic— to become an insurance man in his father's business, I judged him harshly. I just didn't value that as an occupation. I felt a great loss when he made that decision."

Learning to gauge our personal success by our spouse's career success is definitely woven into the tapestry of our traditional socialization process. Perhaps an even stronger thread, however, is our identification with our children's level of success. We celebrate their accomplishments and feel the pain of their defeats. One mother, divorced with two sons, expresses this trait vividly:

> "As a mother you celebrate so much, as I have with my sons. This is just a very normal human trait. And yes, I admit that when my son was earning awards for his painting, I did measure my success as a mother by his accomplishments. I thought, 'I did a pretty good job with him. He inherited some of his talent from me.' Of course, I would never say that to him."

If we are mothers, we can most likely identify with this mother's sense of pride in her child's success as well the self-effacing nature of her last comment. While she is willing to take credit internally, she isn't comfortable taking any credit openly for her son's success.

On the other hand, when our children are failing to meet our expectations, we examine ourselves critically. This mother's story illustrates how intensely affected we can be by a child's negative performance, and how we tend to automatically attribute it to our divorce:

> "I knew there was something terribly wrong with my sixteen year old. He was angry, depressed—acting out. There was no controlling him. I had recently remarried and moved to Washington, D.C. I vividly recall the night I found him a friend's house when he didn't come home at his curfew. He had been drinking, and was very sick. I held his head up through the night to keep him from choking on his own vomit. Words cannot discribe my excruciating pain and sense of failure. I felt so guilty about all that I had put him through over the past five years."

Our identities as Nice Women are firmly rooted in the fact that we personalize the successes and failures of our family members. It is no wonder, then, that when our marriages fail and our families are broken apart in the aftermath of divorce, we feel that we've lost a part of ourselves.

Now that we've discussed these ten prominent expectations, values, and beliefs that Nice Women share regarding marriage and family, what can we conclude? When we contrast them with the messages of the women's movement of the last two decades, they may seem naive. Yet the fact that they are still very much a part of our makeup cannot be disputed.

Why do these beliefs, expectations, and values persist? Haven't we already outlived many of these enchanted notions about "being taken care of" and "saving our marriages," "keeping our families together" and living vicariously through our husband's success? After all, divorce is a fact of life for nearly half of us, so why don't we just accept it and forget the fairytale notion of "happily ever after?"

The answer is that it's just not that simple. The values, beliefs, and expectations upon which we have constructed our lives are not superficial. We didn't build a "house of straw" that could be quickly rebuilt after being blown away. We built our belief system brick by brick, and we built it to last.

As a result, when we find ourselves confronted with the realities of divorce, we are grossly unprepared. We are consumed with intense anxiety and inner conflict. On the surface, divorce is difficult and painful enough, but on a much deeper lever, divorce destroys the traditional matrix which has shaped our lives. Our very identity is splintered as our expectations of marriage and family, emotional and financial security are set adrift. We are suddenly faced with an incredible challenge; perhaps the greatest challenge of our lives.

The exercise at the end of this chapter is designed to help you identify those beliefs, values, and expectations that have had the greatest impact on your life. The goal of this exercise is to help you get to know yourself better and to understand those influences that have shaped you into becoming the Nice Woman you are today.

EXERCISES FOR SELF-DISCOVERY

Measuring the Influence of Traditional Values and Beliefs in our Development as Nice Women

Review each of the following traditional characteristics or beliefs regarding marriage and family. Rate each one on a scale of

5—1 according to how much of an impact it has had on your attitudes. Circle the appropriate number based on the following criteria:

5 points	*very true of me*
4 points	*often true of me*
3 points	*occasionally true of me*
2 points	*rarely true of me*
1 point	*never true of me*

The Ten Characteristics

1. Nice Women have often seen their parents endure long-lasting marriages—many reaching their fortieth or fiftieth wedding anniversaries.

5 4 3 2 1

2. Nice Women have grown up believing they would marry, have children, and live "happily ever after."

5 4 3 2 1

3. Nice Women fantasized as little girls about being taken care of emotionally and financially by strong, protective husbands.

5 4 3 2 1

4. Nice Women have seen friends, acquaintances, and siblings go through divorce and secretly thought it would never happen to them.

5 4 3 2 1

5. Nice Women value keeping their families intact.

5 4 3 2 1

6. Nice Women fight to save their marriages at all costs, believing that if they try hard enough, love enough, understand enough, forgive enough, or change enough, they can make their marriages work.

5 4 3 2 1

7. Nice Women rate highly the needs of their children and husband, putting them above their own.

5 4 3 2 1

8. Nice Women worry the most about how divorce will affect their children.

5 4 3 2 1

9. Nice Women are Super Wives, Super Moms, Super Women.

5 4 3 2 1

10. Nice Women often gauge their success by the success of their husband and/or children.

5 4 3 2 1

Add up your score to determine how much you have been influenced by traditional feminine beliefs regarding marriage and family. The higher your score, the stronger the influence, and the greater your conflict with divorce and the divorce process.

If your score is:

10—20   Overall, you are not greatly influenced by
                 these beliefs, although certain ones may have
                 had an impact on you.

21—35   In general, these beliefs have influenced you.
                 Certain ones may have had more of an effect than
                 others.

36—50   These beliefs have definitely and significantly
                 influenced your attitudes on marriage and family.

Three

Voices That Shaped Us

As little girls, our minds were like sponges. We soaked up all of the attitudes, feelings, and behaviors of our parents and the parent figures in our lives, and both consciously and unconsciously incorporated many of them into our own personalities.

These ways of thinking, seeing, feeling and doing that we absorbed from our parents and other influences were strong factors in determining the women we are today. These messages became a dialogue of voices in our heads. They not only planted the seeds of our self-concept; they also set the rules by which we live our lives. They reflect all of the traditions which have been passed on from generation to generation in our families, and in society as a whole.

Our attitudes about marriage, family, divorce, male and female roles, religion, childrearing, and lifestyles are influenced by these voices from our past. When these voices downgrade women for some behaviors and put them on a pedestal for others, we may do the same thing and not be aware of it. If these social messages supported our dependency and status as "the weaker sex," we most likely absorbed these beliefs at an early age.

As traditional women, we experience a deluge of conflicting voices regarding divorce and its effect on our lives. These voices are accompanied by a myriad of ambivalent feelings and behaviors that are rooted in guilt, fear, and denial. As a result, understanding childhood messages is especially important for Nice Women facing divorce. It allows us to discover how we got to be Nice Women in the first place, and to objectively examine the attitudes we have about ourselves and our capabilities.

The Patterns of Our Voices

If we examine the voices in our heads carefully—that is, if we actually list them and categorize them—we find that for most of us, they fall into several common patterns. An understanding of these patterns and their source is an important step in understanding our conflicts surrounding divorce.

We have all internalized a set of *nurturing voices* to one degree or another. These are the loving, caring, protecting voices that soothed us and sympathized with our physical and emotional hurts. These voices taught us empathy, caring, and encouraged safety and caution. We are responding to our nurturing voices when we care for ourselves, our children, our aging parents, or any other significant people in our lives.

In my workshops on divorce, participants are asked to recall as many nurturing voices or messages as they can from their childhood experiences. When they do, their recollections are most often accompanied by a feeling or behavior. Examples of their responses reveal some interesting patterns. In one such workshop, each woman who shared them began with "I recall...":

"...my mother's soothing voice when I was sick and she fed me chicken soup."

"...being told 'don't get your dress dirty.'"

"...my grandpa singing 'This is the way the ladies ride' as he bounced me on his knee."

"...my father saying 'You're daddy's little girl,' after tucking me in bed."

"...being told not to play with the boys anymore after they pushed me down."

"...my father patting my head and telling me I was his 'little princess'."

"...my father running behind me calling 'Be careful... don't fall...' as I rode my new bike for the first time."

As this group of women analyzed their answers, one of them made an insightful observation: "Most of our nurturing memories take place within our families, either with our parents or grandparents."

Another woman added a different insight. As she reviewed the nuturing messages from the group, it seemed to her that our mothers and fathers expressed these messages in the context of traditional sex roles. That is to say, our mothers were tending to our needs, and our fathers were protecting their little girls.

The other women agreed, and the group reached a consensus. For most of us, nurturing messages were given within the context of our traditional families, and so we associate nurturing messages with the traditional family scenario.

The fact that many of the nurturing voices the women recalled were linked to a type of protectiveness determined by traditional sex roles was also significant. "Don't get dirty," "don't play rough," and "don't take risks" were much more common messages for most us than for our male siblings. While protective messages are an essential part of healthy nurturing, overprotective messages may have prevented us from experiencing some of the frustrations and discomforts that must accompany growth. Sometimes that growth involves skinned knees, bike spills, or climbing too high, rather than being careful and keeping our clothes clean.

At the end of this workshop session, it was apparent that several women had not shared any nurturing recollections. One woman expressed her feelings this way:

> "I just can't recall very many times I felt nurtured. I can remember hearing 'Don't cry'...'don't whine'...'don't be a nuisance,' but I just don't remember being cared for in that way or feeling especially protected. When I heard your recollections, I felt cheated and sad."

It is a fact that the nurturing voices vary for each of us. They may run the gamut from overnurturing and overprotecting to little or no nurturing at all. The collection of nurturing voices that we have depends on our own unique experiences as a child, and the nurturing—or lack of nurturing—that we received.

Another category of voices that often replay in our heads consists of those laced with *criticism*. These messages can be blatant or very subtle, but in either case they are very destructive to our self-esteem. They often have an underlying tone of rigidity, judgmentalism, or blame. They can be prejudicial or unnecessarily prohibitive, or may simply be very opinionated statements which are expressed as fact. They reflect a traditional perspective of what little girls *should* be like. But we must remember that the word "traditional" simply means what has been handed down or what has gone before. These messages we received are usually based on what has been passed on through generations, not on current reality or even common sense.

If our parents and our religious, educational, and media influences communicated traditional or sterotyped beliefs regarding women, our own critical voices are likely to be loaded with such opinions or messages. They influence our values on marriage, family, and religion, as well as our perspectives on traditional female roles and role expectations. The critical inner recordings of Nice Women often replay like this:

"A woman should stick by her man no matter what."

"Divorce is a sin against God."

"Little girls should be sweet and nice."

"A real lady never swears."

"The man is the head of the house."

"A woman who has been divorced twice is a two time loser."

"Children are the real victims of divorce."

"There's nothing worse than an aggressive woman."

"Don't act too smart."

"Men are attracted to women who act like little girls."

"It's a man's world."

"A woman place is in the home."

"Don't argue...don't talk back."

"A good wife and mother makes sacrifices for her family."

I could go on and on with this list of sterotypes posing as "rules," because it is unending. Nice Women never have any difficulty recalling an abundance of such messages, partly because the social messages we receive even now often reflect such opinions. Even in the 1990s, when many of us feel that these dictums sound outdated, we must remember that they were taught to us when we were Nice little girls, and that we soaked them up and incorporated them into our own self-images at an impressionable age. At some level of our inner self, we still buy into many of these "rules" which continue to have a negative impact on our self-concept and limit our choices.

A good way to recognize our voices of criticism is to become aware of our "shoulds." The influence of these messages is what psychologist Karen Horney calls the "tyranny of the shoulds." For Nice Women, the "shoulds" replay especially loudly when our marriages begin to unravel:

"I *should* be a supportive wife."

"I *should* be a perfect mother."

"I *should* endure this marriage for the sake of my children."

"I *should* keep my family intact."

"I *should* keep a clean house like my mother did."

"I *should* be able to solve the problems in my marriage."

"I *should* keep a happy face on for the sake of my children."

"I *should* be able to juggle work and family demands."

(You can probably add your own unique "shoulds" to this list.)

Our "shoulds" are actually a litany of traditional concepts that we, as Nice little girls, incorporated into our behaviorial expectations. If our parenting was especially traditional, our "should" list is likely to be deeply ingrained in us. When our "should" list conflicts with our reality, as in the case of divorce, the result is inner turmoil and accompanying guilt.

Conflict and guilt are evident throughout the stories of the Nice Women in Chapter Two who shared their struggles to act according to their traditional beliefs on marriage and family. It is no wonder that when we understand the "shoulds" that have influenced us, we also recognize that Nice Women experience a significant inner conflict when faced with the realities of divorce.

Another type of negative critical voice that we need to recognize is the kind that manifests itself as "black/white" or "either/or" messages. We can identify these messages through their use of all encompassing words such as "always" or "never":

"Your father and I *always*..."

"A lady *never*..."

"Children of divorce *always*..."

"In our family we've *never*..."

When we evaluate ourselves and our experiences in these "all or nothing" terms, we are replaying voices of criticism which are rigid and guilt-provoking. As a result, we may experience situations as all good or all bad rather than being open to more tolerant shades of gray. "Black/white" messages often replay like this:

"Women *always* talk too much."

"He *never* loved me."

"We've *never* had a divorce in this family."

"We'll *never* be able to get through this."

"You should *always* have the upper hand."

"I'll *never* trust you again."

"You'll *never* forgive yourself."

"I'll *never* make it on my own."

This type of polar thinking is rooted in a naive view of the world rather than in a realistic assessment of the way it really is. Divorce is not a "black or white" issue, and the fallout from it—emotionally, financially, and otherwise—involves many gray areas. In order to reduce our guilt and inner conflict during the divorce process, it is important that we learn to identify the inflexible assumptions which often replay in our heads. Then, in time, we can replace them with a more accurate and realistic appraisal of our situation.

There is another major collection of voices that Nice Women need to be particularly aware of. These are the voices that *give us permission to be less than we are capable of being.* These voices may have come from a well-meaning parent or other caretaker, such as a grandparent or older sibling, whose overprotectiveness encouraged us to be too dependent, passive, or fearful. Most often they treated us this way under the auspices of love.

The term "codependent behavior" refers to the behavior of a partner that allows or encourages the unhealthy or dependent behavior of the other person in the relationship. The person who facilitates the other's unhealthy behavior is referred to as the "enabler." The limiting (or enabling) voices inside of us work in much the same way, replaying messages that reinforce our helplessness, dependency, and passivity.

Our limiting voices are often subtle and difficult to identify. The messages may sound supportive or sympathetic, but rather than encourage our independence, they really invite *dependence.* Often they undermine our feelings of competency and suggest that we may fail. Nice Women are likely to recall messages like these:

"That math looks hard. I never did get math when I was in school."

"You look so tired. Why don't you just stay home?"

"Are you sure you're ready for that? It looks awfully hard to me."

"I've always been afraid to drive on the freeway."

"You'll always be daddy's little girl."

"I never finished college, and I did all right."

"That teacher expects too much from you."

"I guess there's nothing more you can do."

"How on earth will you manage?"

"Someday your prince will come."

"Make sure you marry a rich man the next time."

If we analyze these messages carefully, we can detect an overtone which encourages us to "smooth things over" or "make life easier" for ourselves. If we follow this "advice" consistently from childhood to adulthood, we develop a low tolerance for frustration, and the more frustrated we feel, the lower our self-esteem becomes.

If we examine the last two messages, we can detect another subtlety. Magical thinking emerges as a theme—a belief that someone, somewhere, somehow, will rescue us. What is clearly missing in these negative messages is the belief that progress and change come through our own initiative, hard work, and perseverance.

We must also remember that messages were not all that we internalized; we also absorbed the behaviors we observed. If our parental role models fit the traditional masculine/feminine roles, we most likely observed our mothers engaging in more passive, dependent behaviors. The very structure of the traditional family enabled our mothers to play out this role. Nice Women recall observing the following sterotyped roles and behaviors in their parents:

Mother was a homemaker.

Father was the breadwinner.

Mother rarely confronted father.

Father "ruled the roost."

Mother called her husband "daddy" or "father."

Father managed the money.

Mother never took a trip alone.

Father did the disciplining.

Mother put her own needs last.

Father made important decisions.

Many Nice Women who reached adulthood in the 50s, 60s, and 70s claim to have rejected the traditional role they observed their mothers playing. Yet in their own marriages, they often admit that they allowed these role expectations to resurface and automatically began to conform to them.

In their book, *Women As Winners: A Guide to Understanding, Growth, and Authenticity*, authors Dorothy Jongeward and Dru Scott point out that as women we were just as influenced by our childhood *perceptions* of our parents' roles as we were by any direct messages we received. This is borne out by the large number of Nice Women who forfeited college degrees and job security to become traditional wives and mothers, much like their own mothers.

Voices of Encouragement

So far, the voices that we have examined have been more harmful than positive. Still, we have likely had other messages instilled in us that are more encouraging and which teach us how to do things competently and promote the belief that we are capable of becoming autonomous females. This kind of message encourages us to recognize our need for growth and inspires us to take educated risks. It helps us approach problems from a rational, problem-solving perspective, and seek out and explore options for feasible solutions.

Our encouraging messages often originated with a parent or parent figure who accepted the fact that we would make mistakes, and who allowed us to learn from them. Theirs are the voices that provided positive feedback for doing well, and encouraged us as little girls to ask for what we needed. These positive messages molded and shaped our growth, not through criticism or enabling, but through firm, realistic expectations and rational demands for successful performance. These voices taught us to cope with our own day-to-day frustrations without always feeling responsible for the well-being of others.

While conducting a workshop at a community college, I requested that the participants recall as many *encouraging* messages as they could. For the first time, the women at the workshop were at a loss for words. I reminded them that these messages could have come from anyone we perceived as having authority: parents, stepparents, teachers, relatives, ministers, priests—even a valued neighbor or family friend. Here are some examples of encouraging messages. As you read through them, you will notice that some of them affirm feelings, some set limits, and others encourage practical problem-solving solutions.

"I bet you can figure out a solution to your problem."

"I'll be here if you need help."

"It's okay to speak up for what you need."

"All friends have disagreements sometimes. You can talk it over and still be friends."

"I liked the way you solved that problem."

"I can see that you're angry."

"No, you can't drop your math class. Let's arrange for you to get some tutoring."

"Don't pull the kitten's tail—he may scratch you. I'll show you how to hold him gently."

"I can see that you are frustrated. It takes time to learn a new skill."

"This is a difficult problem. Let's break it into smaller pieces."

"You really used your head."

"You seem unclear about your chores. Let's make a list to get organized."

"Some things are not in our control."

"Good grades are important if you want to go to college. I'll help you set up a study schedule."

"You feel your teacher is being unfair. Let's arrange a conference."

"Think it through before you decide."

After being provided examples like these, a few of the women were able to recall similar messages in their own lives. However, it was difficult for most of the participants to recall more than one or two such supportive messages which readily replayed when they were confronted with a problem in their present day lives.

Why did so many of our parents and parent figures do so little parenting from this positive, affirming, teaching perspective? The answer most likely lies in the historical roots of traditional parenting and the very structure of the traditional family. For the most part, the traditional parent was not a teaching parent. The most common styles of parenting were the authoritarian style and the passive style. One woman whose parents fell into these categories explained her acceptance of them this way:

> "My parents had a traditional marriage even though my mother was also a professional woman with an excellent job. She used to complain to me about my father's rigid, authoritarian ways, but she never openly confronted him. What he told us to do, we did. We learned rather quickly not to ask why. This was just the way it was— the way it had always been done."

This woman speaks for many of us. She was describing traditional parenting as it had "always been done." Unfortunately, the supportive messages which encourage us to take risks, make decisions, and develop our competencies were not abundant in the recollections of Nice Women raised in traditional homes.

Our traditional feminine socialization is a very powerful force. Understanding it and its messages is vital. *Upon close examination, we discover that nearly every message, feeling, experience, and behavior that was reinforced by our traditional feminine socialization thwarts our growth and competency as women.*

Before, during, and after divorce we must exercise the very competencies, responsibilities, and behaviors that so much of our traditional feminine socialization process has limited. Consequently, we must carefully examine those messages that continue to limit us. We must learn to put aside the mental roadblocks that our well-meaning traditional upbringing has put in our way in order to meet the new emotional and behavioral demands thrust upon us by divorce.

By examining our own messages, we can discover the source of many of the voices which speak to us over and over again. We can also begin to realize that we take many of these messages—positive or negative, nurturing or critical, encouraging or limiting—for granted. By understanding their origin, we can exercise choice; we can decide which to keep and which to discard. We will discover that many of these internalized messages will only hinder us as divorced women.

This process of selection will be fully explored in a later chapter. In the next chapter we will take a look at the impact of our traditional upbringing on the development of our feminine self-concept.

The following exercises are designed to help you recall your own messages from your past and become more aware of how these messages still influence you today. You may wish to write your answers down and return to them from time to time. These exercises, like most of the exercises in this book, also lend themselves to a workshop or discussion format.

EXERCISES FOR SELF-DISCOVERY

Recalling Our Nurturing Messages

Go back over the list of nurturing messages on pages 42-43, and try to recall as many of your own as possible.

Who was your primary nurturer when you were a child? Your mother? Your father? Other parent figures?

What was the general tone of the nurturing you received? Was it warm? Distanced? Protective? Overprotective?

Do you nurture others in the same way? If so, how?

In what ways do you nurture yourself?

Examining Our Stereotyped "Rules"

Review the list of stereotyped "rules" on page 45.

Which ones sound familiar to you?

What were the sources of these "rules?" Parent figures? Religious figures? Social messages?

Do you still believe in any of them today? Which ones?

Do they still influence your opinions about yourself or your divorce? If so, in what way?

Identifying our "Shoulds"

Review the list of "shoulds" on page 46 that have been contributed by various Nice Women. Identify those that are familiar to you.

Do you continue to adhere to these "shoulds" at some level? If so, how?

Next, write down two or three of your own "shoulds," particularly those regarding marriage and family.

How do these "shoulds" affect your feelings surrounding divorce?

Recalling Our "Black/White" Messages

Complete the following phrases with messages from your own experiences, especially those voices that pertain to marriage and family.

"We've never _____."

"You always _____."

"Why do you always _____."

"You should never _____."

Are these messages influential in your life today?

Does part of you still believe these messages to be true?

How could you modify these messages from a "black/white" perspective to a more flexible one?

Recognizing Our Limiting Cues

Review the limiting messages on page 49.

Do some of them sound familiar to you? If so, which ones?

Can you recall specific messages of your own which limit your self-confidence? If so, write them down.

Is there a little girl in you waiting to be rescued? What would you most like to be rescued from?

How do you handle your frustration when situations become difficult?

Again, you may find it helpful to review your written answers periodically. This will help you tune into your limiting voices, which is the only way to become more aware of how they can continue to limit your capabilities.

Four

Through the Looking Glass

Our very first steps towards becoming Nice Women began at birth. From that point on, we learned to adapt to our environment and to the people in it. Through our interactions with parents and parent figures, we began our journeys of adaptation; not only to survive, but also to find a place for ourselves in a very big world.

The ability to adapt to the world around us is necessary to our very survival. The lessons we learn civilize us and provide us with the skills we need to become functioning members of society. Through this socialization process, we learned to get along with others, to take turns, and to become aware of the needs and feelings of others. We developed caution to protect us from dangerous situations. We also learned, much to our chagrin, that we were not the "center of the universe."

This process of adaptation is ongoing throughout our lives. However, it is especially powerful during the first five years. The following behaviors illustrate typical learned responses from early childhood:

- smiling in response to approval

- saying "please" and "thank-you"

- sulking after being punished

- considering the feelings of others

- developing caution towards potential dangers

Unfortunately, in the traditional feminine socialization process, there is a tendency for parents, other figures of authority, and society as a whole, to *overadapt* females. This tendency is rooted in our traditional and historical notions of what constitutes acceptable feminine behavior. As seen in the previous chapters, the childhood experiences of Nice Women support the argument that parental overprotection and enabling are a large part of a traditional feminine upbringing.

We have discussed the importance of becoming aware of the many "shoulds" that have influenced us and supported patterns of overadaptation. "Little girls *should* be quiet and sweet" and "little girls *should* not be aggressive" are messages that are familiar to us all. What we don't always recognize, however, is that we internalized what we heard and adapted our behavior to meet those expectations. More than we'd like to admit, *we became a mirror image of what others expected us to be.*

One of the best ways to understand the power of the adaptive process is to take a look at the unsocialized, natural child that we once were. We can learn much from this spontaneous little creature by examining her behavior and noting how our outlook has changed since we were her age.

Revisiting the Spontaneous Little Girl

The "Wheeee..." of a child joyfully descending a playground slide or the unrestrained, foot-stomping tantrum of a toddler in the supermarket are examples of the uncensored impulses that characterize the unsocialized child. The newborn baby is the epitome of a lack of inhibitions—she cries when she's hungry or wet, coos in pleasure at her mother's breast, and soils her diaper when she feels the urge. Naturally curious, this uninhibited child uses her senses—sight, taste, smell, touch, and hearing—to explore and experience her world. By observing the unrestricted behaviors of infants, we can begin to understand how long and complex our socialization process has been.

As we grow from infancy to the toddler stage, we still retain some of the characteristics of the spontaneous child. We are still impulsive, self-centered, rebellious, and open to sensorial experiences. Some typical behaviors that a young child might engage in are:

- enjoying an ice cream cone lick by lick, unconscious of it dripping on her clothes

- throwing a temper tantrum

- splashing in a puddle

- grabbing the biggest piece of cake

- yelling, biting, or hitting

- running naked on the beach

- declaring "no! I won't!"

- chasing a butterfly

As young children, we may also develop apprehension of certain things. It is not uncommon for young children to fear the dark, strangers, loud noises, such as sirens or fireworks, being dropped or falling, or being abandoned, left or forgotten.

It is through our life experiences that we modify or outgrow our childhood fears. However, if we were overprotected, or if our life experiences actually reinforced our fears, they may remain with us in our adult lives and inhibit the development of our independence.

For example, if we have been abandoned as little girls—either physically or emotionally—we may reexperience this fear of abandonment over and over again in our adult relationships, especially when a marital breakup becomes imminent. We may cling to the institution of marriage with the same intense desperation of the little girl who was dependent on adults to take care of her. *Any unresolved fears or significant losses that we experienced during our early years may continue to influence our behaviors today, including the way we cope with divorce.*

The Shaping of the Nice Little Girl

The uninhibited child exhibits a full range of behaviors—from curiosity to affection to rebelliousness to aggressiveness to fear. If these behaviors are not modified to some degree as we mature, they become obstacles in our adult lives.

For example, if we *always* acted impulsively, we couldn't make long-range plans or set goals. Our lives would be chaotic. Or, if we remained too self-centered, we would repel the love and affection that we desire from those that we care about the most.

On the other hand, if these natural behaviors are squelched completely, or nearly so, we develop patterns of overcompliance, helplessness, and dependency. We lack the emotional tenacity which is vital to functioning independently in the real world.

When Nice Women examine their early childhood experiences regarding assertive behavior, their responses most often reflect an overadaptation against assertiveness. This woman's recollection is typical of many of my workshop participants:

"I remember vividly the time I was asked to pick up my

toys and I rebelliously declared 'No!' to my father. I was spanked and sent to my room. I remember his words as if it were yesterday. 'Don't ever tell me 'No' when I tell you to do something!' I was only three and a half, but I learned at an early age that saying 'No!' got you into trouble, and that being good and doing what you were told made other people happy."

No doubt this woman's father, and the fathers of the other women who relayed similar stories, were functioning in the authoritarian manner that traditional fathers often did, and still do. However, those early messages regarding our right to say "no" or assert ourselves left long-lasting impressions on many of us.

Another woman offered her perspective. She recalled that the pressure to adapt to more feminine roles increased as she grew older:

"As I think about my very early years, I sense that it was okay for me to experience these childlike behaviors to some degree when I was very young. But by the age of four or five, I was expected to begin to act like a little lady. I recall that my brothers got away with much more than I did. Boys were expected to get dirty, or make a mess, or be aggressive, but not girls. I was praised for being polite and helpful."

These women's recollections summarize the feelings of most of the women I have worked with. When given an opportunity to examine their own feminine socialization from this perspective, Nice Women identify with the concept that the process overly restricts our natural spontaneity and inhibits our ability to be assertive.

Uncensored Behavior vs. Overadapted Behavior

One effective way of grasping the importance of allowing the appropriate expression of behaviors in a child is to view them on a continuum—a scale of uncensored to overmodified or squelched behaviors.

The left column in the chart below contains typical behaviors of the uncensored or unsocialized child. The right column represents the overadapted behaviors that result when, rather than being modified, the behaviors of the natural child are squelched. The behaviors in the middle column represent healthy, modified behaviors.

Take a few minutes to review the behaviors and decide on the ones that best describe you at this time in your life.

UNCENSORED BEHAVIOR	*MODIFIED BEHAVIOR*	OVERADAPTED BEHAVIOR
rebellious	*adaptable*	overcompliant
curious	*problem-solving*	detached/ uninvolved
impulsive	*spontaneous*	restrained
self-indulgent	*self-disciplined*	denies own needs
fearful	*cautious*	gullible/naive
aggressive	*assertive*	passive
creative/ expressive	*focused*	self-censoring
self-centered	*sense of self*	self-conscious

Can you identify behaviors you engage in which are self-defeating or overadapted? In which column or columns do the majority of your behaviors fall? Do you see a pattern?

There are no right or wrong answers to this activity. It is simply designed to help you become more aware of your own behaviors, especially those that may be hindering your growth.

Effective, productive behaviors usually fall in a flexible range somewhere in between the two extremes. When we learn to achieve this midpoint as adults, it allows us to establish balance between our overadapted past and the realities and demands of our present lives.

As Nice Women, an *appropriate* expression of our spontaneous, uncensored child is especially important. For example, our ability to engage in spontaneous play depends on our ability to get in touch with the feelings of the spontaneous little girl we once were. If our scale is constantly tipped to the repressed side, we not only deny an important part of ourselves, we also never fully develop or use the skills and behaviors needed to take care of ourselves and those we are responsible for after divorce.

For example, we may need to find a better paying career in a tough job market, or return to school in order to get more training. We will need to exercise some stubbornness and tenacity in order to do so.

We must also learn to deal assertively with lawyers and ex-spouses regarding such issues as child support payments, custody, and visitation. It becomes imperative that we speak up clearly and at times make demands in order to get what we need. We must learn to say "no" clearly and emphatically without feeling guilty. We must become more aware of our own needs in order to preserve the physical and emotional energy that is so quickly depleted under the stress of divorce, single parenting, and financial hardship. Since these behavioral tasks are not automatic to most of us, they must be identified, practiced and strengthened. Our behavior then becomes more a function of choice and less a reaction to our traditional conditioning.

Feminine Expectations and Our Childhood Coping Strategies

There is another aspect of our natural, spontaneous child that we haven't yet examined. Not only was the little girl fearful, aggressive, and self-centered, she was also very clever.

She possessed a kind of unschooled wisdom—an uncanny ability to figure things out. Using intuition, experimentation, and creativity, she figured out how to cope with parental and societal demands and expectations. She became adept at reading people's faces and anticipating other people's needs at a very young age. She figured out that there were ways to get her needs met while avoiding conflict at the same time. As a result, she developed coping strategies or behavioral patterns which, for many of us, became an integral part of our feminine personalities.

We developed a specific set of coping behaviors for many reasons, such as:

- to fulfill our desire to please

- to avoid conflict

- to meet parental or social expectations

- to conform to our perceptions of feminine behavior

- to reflect our birth order in the family, whether we were the oldest, youngest, middle, or only child

- to adapt to a unique family situation such as elderly parents, chronically ill or depressed parents, or the death of a sibling

- to cope with alcholism, physical or emotional abuse, or other dysfunctional circumstances

or, simply, because we felt we had no other choice.

Most of us can relate to one or more of these circumstances. As little girls, we had no control over them. The only choice we had was to adapt to our surroundings and to the needs and expectations of those around us.

Everyone must adapt to some degree, and we must continue to do so as adults; it is a reality of life. Just as when we were a child we had to obey certain rules at home and at school, as an adult we may need to dress up for work, even though we would be more comfortable in jeans. However, if we *almost always* had to adapt, or felt that we did, we may have developed patterns of overadaptation that need to be examined. We must then decide whether they are useful in our adult lives.

Coping Strategies Common to Nice Women

1. Overcompliance

Overcompliance develops when we always—or almost always—do precisely what we are told to do. Overcompliance also manifests itself when we always do what we *perceive* we should do or are expected to do. We may do what we feel is expected of us not because we want to, but rather because *not* doing it produces feelings of guilt or creates inner conflict. Our compliant behavior becomes blind and habitual. It also becomes what feels most familiar.

As adults, Nice Women often comply simply because we lack the skills or confidence to examine other alternatives. Irene, a woman whose traditional childhood had far-reaching effects on her adult life, illustrates this point with the following account:

"I was raised in a strict, religious, traditional home. You did what you were told, and that was that. Later, when I was married, my patterns of compliance were automatic. I had difficulty making decisions. I was depressed much of the time. I felt so stuck. But rather than stopping and asking, 'What's not working here?' I just kept going. I continued to meet everyone's needs, as I had done as a child. I performed all the traditional tasks, as my mother had done.

"Finally, my depression became so severe that I was forced to stop and take stock of my life. I had to get help. Through counseling and self-education, I am finally learning that as an adult I do have choices—choices that I never knew I had as a child."

Irene's story may ring true for you. It does for me. I remember that when I faced the excruciating decisions which surrounded my divorce, I would have gladly accepted the advice of some wise oracle. Compliance was something I understood.

In addition to emphasizing how Nice Women learn to make compliance a habit, Irene's story illustrates another important point: *Depression almost always accompanies childhood patterns of overcompliance.* Over and over again in my workshops and counseling sessions, women facing divorce have shared stories of chronic depression as they've tried to carry out the roles that they feel are expected of them and at the same time make decisions that are healthy for them and their children. Because being divorced does not fit into any of our traditional roles, it compounds our depression, and, coupled with the demands of divorce, creates a vicious, conflicting cycle which can even become life threatening. Mary, a woman whose divorce brought her to the edge of despair, shares her experience:

"It is only now, looking back, that I realize what a dark hole I was really in. I was so depressed; I didn't want to live. I could no longer cope with all of the demands on me and at the same time hang onto a marriage that was so unhealthy.

"On the other hand, the thought of divorce and all of its fallout was just as bleak. It was like being caught in a maze with no way out. If it hadn't been for the fact that my son needed me, I might not have made it. I knew I had to be there for him, so I kept hanging on. Finally, with the help of a skilled therapist and antidepressants, I was slowly able to crawl out of that dark hole. At times I still reexperience the pain of those terrible days."

There are no shortcuts in the journey out of severe depression. It involves introspective work with the help of a skilled counselor or therapist, and sometimes, as in Mary's case, antidepressants can be of help. Regardless of its severity, however, *depression almost always involves unresolved anger or grief, a long list of "shoulds," and a feeling that we are not in control of our lives.* It does not respond to our reliance on old patterns of overcompliance, or our adherence to our "should" list. Sometimes the journey out of this quagmire not only involves divorce, but freeing ourselves from the "shoulds" which surround our divorce as well.

2. Sulking, Withdrawing, and Other Tactics of Avoidance

As little girls, we sometimes found that the use of avoidance tactics, such as sulking or withdrawing, were solutions to problems for which compliance wasn't the answer. The use of these tactics is really the Nice little girl's way of saying, "I can't" or "I won't." This woman who admitted that she always had difficulty saying "no" during her twenty-two year marriage shared her childhood experience with avoidance at a group counseling session:

"I learned that by pouting or sulking I could avoid a parental demand without actually saying 'no.' I would go to my room and stay there, hoping the situation would go away. I discovered that sulking often got me sympathy from my father, and I often ended up getting what I wanted."

It's not unusual for children to try to use avoidance tactics to get themselves out of a jam. You may recall developing a headache or stomachache to avoid a test at school or a piano recital for which you were unprepared. *It is when we routinely use these tactics to avoid confrontation in our adult lives that they become self-defeating.* As with compliance, an overreliance on avoidance strategies in our adult lives may lead to depression.

3. Using Manipulation to Gain Power and Control

Manipulation, often characterized in women as "using our feminine wiles," is considered by many to be a distinctly feminine trait. As little girls, many of us learned quickly how we could best manipulate grownups. Because behavioral expectations often prohibited us from asking for what we wanted directly or from using our physical strength to get it, we discovered other ways of getting the job done.

Perhaps we observed our mother using manipulative tactics in order to gain power in her marriage, as this woman who was recently separated recalls:

"I can remember my mother saying many times with a wink, 'Always remember the golden rule.' This meant that we—my sister and I—shouldn't ask daddy for anything until he had had his cocktail and read the newspaper. Then we would work on him little by little, pretending whatever it was that we wanted was really his idea. If that didn't work, we would snuggle up to him. If that didn't soften him up, we'd turn on the tears."

If we examine our own childhood behaviors, most of us will discover ways in which we manipulated others in order to get our way. After all, many children are very clever when it comes to manipulating adults, playmates, or siblings. This is one way of balancing their relative powerlessness. But, like the other coping strategies, there is a downside.

If we relied heavily on manipulation, we may have developed an unrealistic sense of our own power. Because of our lack of life experiences and our naive perception of cause and effect, *we may have actually come to believe that we have the power to control others and cause them to behave in the ways we want them to behave.*

If we carry this belief into our adult lives unchecked, we may continue to rely on this unrealistic sense of power. We may to try to get our needs met by controlling others, rather than by addressing our own needs in a direct way.

We may try to overly influence the lives of those we love in order to get them to behave as we would like. Unconsciously, we may rely on our leftover childhood perception of our "magical" power to assist us. Of course, we don't consciously say, "I will manipulate this situation to gain power." Like other coping strategies, our behavior is automatic. However, like the little girl we once were, we are still trying to gain power by controlling others.

Unfortunately, the underlying reason that we retain this behavior is that as Nice Women we often feel, consciously or unconsciously, that the use of manipulative tactics *is* necessary to gain power and get our needs met. As has been illustrated through the stories of Nice Women in previous chapters, many of us truly believe that if we try hard enough, love enough, understand enough, forgive enough, or change enough, that we can control the behavior of others, and ultimately the outcome of our marriages.

I believe that what is popularly referred to as "women's

intuition" is in part a finely tuned skill or strategy which we learned early in our lives to please and manipulate others. With no academic knowledge of psychology, the very young child *intuits* the reasons for much of what is going on in her world. She reads faces and interprets tones long before she has developed language. She makes early decisions about her world based on what she can discern, and she quickly learns what actions and behaviors elicit a positive response.

With this in mind, it's not surprising that Nice Women are often highly intuitive. I know that I am. I was, and still am, very good at reading people and predicting situations.

As a child I learned early how to make others happy and avoid conflicts. I observed the various moods of my parents and grandparents. I learned to predict the behavior patterns that would lead to conflict or a family crisis. I actually developed a kind of mental roadmap to know in which directions their moods were going to go. I would clue in my sisters and we would adjust our behavior accordingly. Today, people are often amazed at what they see as my strong sense of intuition—of knowing what is going to happen.

The majority of Nice Women I've spoken with share similar stories of their "powers of intuition." Actually, our finely honed intuition can be a useful tool when we couple it with reliable information. However, if we use it strictly to gain power or to cleverly control others, it becomes negative and self-defeating.

4. Denial of Unpleasant Feelings—Especially Anger

As we grew up, we became aware that certain expressions of feelings or displays of behavior were tolerated, and certain ones were not. In many traditional families, outbursts of anger or displays of aggressiveness were the least tolerated from little girls. Unfortunately, what many of us didn't learn was an acceptable alternative. How could we express anger or frustration in acceptable ways? What we often did learn (and became very good at) was repressing our negative feelings of anger or hostility.

In the counseling I have done with adolescents, the repression of anger is a very common issue. What happens quite often when anger is not expressed is that it comes out "sideways," often in a self-destructive manner. For example, repressed anger in young women often expresses itself through depression, eating disorders, promiscuity, or other self-destructive behaviors. Sometimes it can lead to contemplation of suicide, or even suicide attempts.

The automatic repression of anger is not uncommon for Nice Women. In my workshops and counseling sessions, women have shared their experiences with chronic depression, drinking or smoking too much, fad dieting or binging, and thoughts of suicide as they tried to come to terms with the failure of their marriages.

5. Denial of Self and the Importance of One's Own Needs

"Selfish behavior," or attitudes or displays of what was perceived as selfishness by females, were also not tolerated in most traditional families. We were praised for thinking of others and taking care of the needs of others. The behavior of our role models—our mothers and grandmothers—also reinforced this behavior. Consequently, many of us lost the meaning of *self* in the caretaking of others, even though we may have gone through periods of egocentricity or self-centeredness as young children and adolescents.

Along with this need to cater to others, many of us developed a very stong sense of responsibility for the welfare of family members. This was particularly true if we were an older or oldest child, had male siblings, or had a parent that was physically or emotionally handicapped.

The very structure of the traditional family reinforced this caretaking behavior. Nice Women often recall an emotionally distant father who carried out the "breadwinner" role, and a mother who was needy and dependent.

Many Nice Women also remember handling their family responsibilities efficiently and reaping great praise for their accomplishments. This was certainly true for me. As an older daughter in a large family, I routinely cared for the needs of my younger siblings, and I was very good at it.

I recall an occasion at age sixteen when my parents were scheduled to attend a convention out of town. I actually begged to be left in charge. For five days I cooked, cleaned, and did laundry for my six younger siblings. I set up a chore schedule and rewarded them with gold stars for good work. I packed lunches and drove them to school on time. No wonder I felt so confident and capable when I began running my own home and family. I had been in training throughout my childhood!

I have talked with many Nice Women over the years who were oldest or older daughters among their siblings, only daughters in a family of male children, or in some cases, only children. They often have shared similar stories from their own family experiences.

It wasn't until much later in my married life that I realized the negative fallout that resulted from such an overdeveloped sense of responsibility. For me, the consequence of these early caretaking experiences was the automatic denial of my own needs. The needs of my husband and children were always my first priority. I assumed that the caretaking role that I had carried out as a child would also work for me in my role as wife and mother. It has taken me a long time to figure out why it simply would not work out the same way in my adult life.

6. Patterns of Perfectionism

Because there was so much emphasis on doing rather than being in out lives, Nice little girls learned to do many things well. Perhaps you can remember being praised for doing a job "perfectly" or being made to redo a chore until it was "perfect." Typically, the expectations of our traditional parents were high. As little girls, we worked hard to meet them in order to reap the rewards of praise for a "perfect" job.

Many of us were good students in elementary school, and although academic achievements were rewarded less and less as we got older, we continued our patterns of perfectionism as we moved through the stages of our development. We had to look perfect, act perfect, and have the perfect boyfriend.

We looked to *Seventeen, Glamour,* and *Mademoiselle* for models of feminine beauty, which for most of us, of course, were unattainable. Many of our feelings of self-worth were tied to the feedback we received from others, on our looks as well as on our efforts. If we didn't receive the feedback we wanted, we tried harder. We knew it was out there somewhere, and we were determined to get it. We just weren't satisfied with anything less than perfection.

I'm what you might call a "recovering perfectionist." My patterns of perfectionism go back to the little girl who felt she could and should do everything perfectly. I was an "A" student, a fine cello player, and a blue ribbon horseback rider. I could cook and clean for a family of twelve and run a household like a professional. The perfectionistic lens through which I viewed myself and the world was so much a part of me that I was completely unaware of its existence.

Later in my life, I found that I was disappointed if an event that I had planned, such as my child's bithday party or a family vacation, was less than perfect. My expectations were outrageously high, but I wasn't aware of it or the toll it was taking.

Anything less than my very best effort wasn't acceptable to me. As a result, others also learned to expect "great things" from me, and I in turn felt added pressure to meet their expectations.

When my son was born I was running the Montessori School near Chicago which I mentioned in the Introduction. He arrived in mid-August, and I never missed a beat. I came home from the hospital, breast-fed him while conducting staff workshops, and opened the fall classes with him snuggled in a pack on my chest. I would dismiss the morning classes at 11:15 and head home by 11:45, nursing him in the car on the way. My staff was amazed at my stamina. They hailed my efforts to stay totally involved in the school. In their eyes, I was the perfect working mother!

Because of my perfectionistic view, however, I had no idea what I was doing, or more importantly, why I was doing it. I was so out of tune with my own needs that I didn't realize the price I was paying for such perfectionism. I ignored my chronic fatigue. I felt guilty because I wasn't acting like the perfect mother for my daughter, who was twelve. I was blind to the problems that were developing in my marriage. The treadmill was running at high speed, and I felt powerless to slow it down.

Only through my divorce, the subsequent pain, and the self-searching and growth I have undergone since have I learned how to tune into my own needs and relax my perfectionism. However, because my early conditioning was so powerful, I still have to work with these tendencies nearly every day in order to keep my life in balance.

The Implications of Our Coping Strategies

The coping strategies that we learned as children are not "wrong" or "bad," but when used to excess or in unhealthy ways, they can have self-defeating effects on our adult lives. As women facing divorce or as women learning to cope with the ramifications of divorce, it is important that we reexamine these coping strategies and decide which ones we need to modify, and which ones we need to discard.

Of course, there are still times when we must comply even though we don't want to, or choose not to express our anger in order to avoid a confrontation. We may have to put our needs on hold periodically in order to help a friend or meet the needs of our children. There are even times when it's best for us to manipulate our way through a situation in order to avoid a conflict. *It is only when these coping strateqies are relied on consistently or are triggered unconsciously that they have a negative effect on our self-esteem.* Rather than us controlling them, they control us— much like my addiction to perfectionism.

An overreliance on our childhood coping strategies also contributes to a self-image that is tentative and vulnerable. Rather that having a self that originates from within, we develop an externalized self—a self that is constantly looking outward to get the feedback and approval that it needs. We validate our self-worth *externally*, just as we did as children.

When we develop an externalized self, the world becomes a mirror that reflects our self-image. When the objects in the mirror fall apart, so do we. When our marriages fail, we are devastated. *To better understand how this happens, we need to consider that from the time we were little girls, we learned to define ourselves by the reflections of marriage and family we viewed in our mirror, not from a self-image that we had developed from within.*

Our sense of self-worth developed as we performed those behaviors which earned us positive reinforcement. As a result, some of us became caretakers who developed an overblown sense of responsibility for others. Some of us became skillful at masking our true feelings, never understanding why we felt depressed. We wore "happy" masks and put our own needs on hold. In fact, some of us became so skilled at anticipating and meeting the needs of others that we ultimately lost sight of our own.

At a career assessment workshop which was designed to help divorcing women zero in on new career options, a woman who was divorcing just as her last child graduated from high school summed up what many other women in the workshop were feeling:

> "I'm supposed to discover what it is that I really want to do for me? After twenty years of being a wife and mother, I'm supposed to discover some "new me?" We had plans that when the kids were gone we would finally have some time and money to travel or remodel the house. Now I'm supposed to discover some new career that's supposed to fulfill me and enable me to support myself. Frankly, I haven't a clue who I am without my marriage and family, or what I want, and I'm really not interested in finding out."

Can you blame her? She didn't plan to be forty years old and have to redesign some new plan for her life. She had spent twenty years preparing to become a wife and mother, and twenty more years in that role. She felt victimized, and understandably so. Many of us have felt that way. Our roles were set, and even if we worked outside our homes, we still defined ourselves by our perceptions of marriage and family that we had learned growing up.

But the realities of divorce change all that. Divorce devastates every traditional expectation regarding marriage and family that we ever had. The old roles no longer suffice. Unless we choose to remain victimized, we are forced to confront the realities of divorce, and our lives will never be the same. In the next chapter we will examine the realities of divorce and the divorce process, and the impact that they have on us as traditional women.

The exercises that follow are designed to help you become aware of how you may still be overrelying on your childhood coping strategies. You will also get a clearer picture of some of the behaviors related to those strategies that may be hindering your growth.

EXERCISES FOR SELF-DISCOVERY

Assessing Our Childhood Coping Strategies

Taking an honest look at how we may be continuing to use our childhood coping strategies is an important step toward developing healthier, more productive behaviors. Answer the following questions as honestly as you can. Your answers will provide some important insights for growth and change.

For each of the questions listed under the coping strategies, give yourself a score of **1, 2**, or **3** points. A **1** indicates that you **rarely** experience this behavior; **2** means that you behave in this way **fairly often**; **3** indicates that you **usually** experience this behavior. We will analyze what our scores mean at the end of the exercise.

1. Blind Compliance

Do you find yourself saying "yes" and later wishing   1 2 3
you had said "no?"

Do you have difficulty saying "no" and sticking to   1 2 3
it?

Do you feel guilty when you say "no"?   1 2 3

2. Sulking, Withdrawing, and Avoidance

Do you find yourself sulking or pouting when you   1 2 3
don't get your needs met?

Do you withdraw from situations in order to avoid   1 2 3
conflict?

3. Manipulation

Do you resort to a roundabout way of getting what   1 2 3
you need—be it from your children, spouse,
ex-spouse, relatives, or people in general?

Do you have difficulty being direct about what you   1 2 3
want or need?

4. Denial of Feelings, Especially Anger

Do you avoid angry confrontations in order to keep   1 2 3
the peace?

Do you feel guilty after expressing anger?   1 2 3

Do you automatically wear a "happy" mask rather   1 2 3
than show unpleasant feelings?

Do you experience feelings of depression?   1 2 3

Do you overeat, drink or smoke too much, or   1 2 3
participate in other types of addictive or
self-destructive behaviors?

5. Denial of Your Own Needs

Do you put the needs of others before your own?   1 2 3

Do you feel angry when you deny your own needs,   1 2 3
but feel that you have no choice?

Do you have trouble identifying what your own   1 2 3
needs are?

6. Perfectionistic Tendencies

Do you feel especially disappointed when things   1 2 3
don't turn out the way you planned?

Do you feel pressure to meet the expectations of   1 2 3
others?

Do you apologize for things not being "good   1 2 3
enough?"

Do you feel you should be able to find solutions to   1 2 3
all your problems?

Now take a look at your answers. Note all of the 2s and 3s that you have circled. These are the things that you feel *fairly often* or *usually* experience.

Under which coping strategies do you have at least one 2 or 3 circled? Put an asterisk (*) next to the coping strategies under which you have circled one or more 2 or 3. The asterisk marks a childhood coping strategy on which you may still be overrelying.

After identifying these coping strategies which may be problem areas, think about how you may have developed these patterns of behavior.

Can you recall situations in your childhood which would have encouraged you to develop an overreliance on these coping strategies? If so, what were they?

Do you feel your reliance on these strategies and their accompanying behaviors hinders your growth? If so, in what ways?

We can tune into our use of childhood coping strategies by examining ourselves and by becoming more positively self-centered and more aware of our overreliance on our automatic behaviors. A good way to begin is to evaluate their usefulness in our present lives. We can ask ourselves: Is this behavior getting me what I really need or want in my life now? We can clarify what makes us feel good and what causes us to feel frustrated, and take control of our behavioral responses. When we are committed to changing our ingrained coping behaviors, we become our own best critic and our own best friend.

Five

The Challenges We Face

Divorce has an impact on every aspect of our lives. Nothing is left untouched by the process of dissolving a marriage. It affects our self-esteem, our children, our extended families, our faith or spirituality, our emotional and financial security, our social life, and our home and family life, not to mention our feelings about the traditions and values with which we were raised. The complexities of divorce are far-reaching, and are with us for the rest of our lives.

The Cycle of Grieving

One of the most difficult aspects of the process begins long before the actual divorce proceedings, as the seeds of marital dissolution are sown. Unresolved anger, values clashes, financial hardships, dishonesty, and infidelity are only a few of the problems which may have surfaced in our daily lives. As these "seeds" germinate, they produce a cycle of frustration and depression that is similar to the cycle of grief that Elisabeth Kubler-Ross describes in her books on death and dying. When someone dies, however, their physical presence is gone, and one must ultimately try to accept the reality of their absence. In the case of divorce, the cycle of grief may repeat itself many times. This is especially true if we continually try to resuscitate our marriage, refusing to admit that it may have died long ago.

This cycle of grief includes different emotional stages or stations that we visit for varying periods of time. These stages, which can return again and again, are *anger, depression, ambivilance, magical thinking, denial, bargaining, and resolution.* The order in which we visit these stages depends on our own individual psychological needs. Progressing through each station involves emotional work that is an inherent part of the grieving process.

Anger includes all of our behavior that blames our spouse, God, the other woman, or a myriad of other "reasons" for the failure of our marriages. We may rant and rave, accuse, lash out at innocent parties, and carry on hysterically out of fear and frustration. In our anger, we ask questions for which there are no easy answers, but demand them anyway in our efforts to gain control. Questions such as "Why did you...?" "How could you...?" " Why can't we...?" echo over and over again.

Although anger may rage inside of us, most Nice Women have difficulty sustaining an outward expression of anger, because it does not mesh with our feminine socialization. Most of us are much more comfortable with internalizing our anger, because it is a coping strategy that feels more familiar. However, as mentioned earlier, internalizing our anger often results in depression and its accompanying feelings of helplessness and despair. For many of us, this stage of grieving replicates our childhood feelings of not being heard, not being loved, or not having our want and needs validated.

Ambivalence has a way of interweaving itself through both the pre- and postdivorce stages of grieving. Naturally, feeling two ways about something generates inner feelings of conflict and anxiety. This is especially true for Nice Women who value the institution of marriage but realize that their own marriage isn't working.

I recall a long-distance conversation I had with one of my sisters a few years ago. I was reaching out, as I often did, for ways to keep my marriage going, even though the events of the previous years made that nearly impossible. With her usual patience, she said, "You need to understand that you can feel two ways about something. That doesn't make either way right or wrong—just different. You may never fully resolve your desire to stay married and the inevitability of your divorce."

Because I was trying so hard to resolve my conflict, I didn't react well to her words at that time, but I came to realize that she was right. Hers was one of those pithy truths that someone says just when you need to hear it. To this day I periodically replay the same conflict I was feeling then. Perhaps I always will.

As you might expect from the previous chapter, *magical thinking* plays an important role in the experiences of Nice Women. We believe that if we try hard enough, we can make our marriages turn out the way we want them to. As we learned earlier, this belief stems from our childhood sense of omnipotence, a naive belief that we have the power to make all things work the way we want them to. Consequently, most of us have engaged in one or more of the following behaviors in order to avoid facing divorce as the only option:

- We have made numerous adjustments in ourselves and in our role as wives.

- We have tried to change our spouses.

- We have been in and out of counseling, either individually or as a couple.

- We have seesawed between the possibility of separation or divorce and trying to save our marriages.

- We have consulted an attorney or even completed a
  separation agreement without filing it.

- We have actually filed a divorce petition, only to
  withdraw it as the court date grew near.

- We have separated and reconciled more than once,
  only to reexperience the grief cycle all over again.

The difference between magical thinking behaviors and
productive strategies is that in the case of the former, we keep
trying and hoping to make things work out even though there are
no real changes taking place.

Denial also plays a role in the grieving cycle, protecting us
from those feelings or realities that are too painful to fully
acknowledge. For Nice Women, the reality of divorce is often
so painful that denial becomes a very powerful force, as the
following story illustrates. Ellen, a gentle, softspoken woman of
forty-two, shared her story with me during an interview:

"Looking back, it's hard to believe how ironclad my
denial system was. There were so many signs along the
way that I simply could not or would not see. The most
blatant example of my denial was my refusal to see that
he was having an affair. He began to travel more, to stay
away on weekends, to spend less and less time at home.
The strange thing about my denial was that even though
I refused to consciously confront the signs, my emotional
energy became more and more depleted. My moods
swung between outbursts of anger and feeling guilty for
behaving that way. I was sure my outrageous behavior
was driving him further away. When I finally realized
that he *was* having an affair, it came to me like an
intuitive flash. All of the pieces suddenly fit! I know
now that my denial was protecting me from the incredible

pain that engulfed me when I finally realized the truth."

Denial does serve a protective purpose. However, if we are perpetually stuck in denial, not seeing things as they really are and not allowing ourselves to feel things, we risk cutting ourselves off from experiencing other aspects of life, including joy. Unacknowledged and unprocessed pain can remain a very powerful force in our lives, and will often manifest itself in more harmful ways. If our fear of feeling pain becomes too great, we may need to seek the help of a skilled therapist in order to work through it.

In the *bargaining* stage, we make promises and compromises in order to keep our marriages and our families together. We may promise to be better at something, or to stop doing something. In exchange, we may ask our spouse to make a renewed effort to work things out, or he may ask for whatever it is he feels he needs in order to stay in the marriage.

Of course, healthy compromise is an important part of any relationship. It is when we compromise too many of our own needs that this stage becomes dysfunctional. As one woman told me, "It finally got to the point that all I asked of him was to pay his taxes and not cheat on me anymore. I was willing to settle for that in order to keep our family together!"

Each time we engage in one of these stages, we're seeking a new way of coping. We may go from denial, to bargaining, and then into magical thinking. When our new strategy fails, we may plunge into depression or escalate into anger. But regardless of how we move through the stages, we feel stuck each time they repeat themselves.

Rachel's story may sound familiar to you. Here she is talking about her second divorce, which for many Nice Women is often much more difficult than the first:

"As early as 1982, right after our son was born, I knew

something was terribly wrong. On the inside our marriage was crumbling, though we were perceived by our friends and our church as the perfect couple. I tried every strategy I could think of to pull us out of this very dark hole. I helped with his business and managed his office. We went into marital couseling and individual couseling for at least three years. When my strategies had run the gamut, I became very depressed. But then I would develop another plan and start all over again, hoping something would work out. I was determined not to let my second marriage end in divorce, as my first one had. It wasn't until 1989 that our divorce was final."

The process of making a decision to end a marriage is a long and agonizing experience. Each Nice Woman seems to have her own unique pattern and time frame. Certainly no one else can decide our timing for us. But unless we are able to remain on this debilitating merry-go-round indefinitely, we will ultimately have to take action of some kind.

In most cases, an eruption finally occurs that causes the intensity of the stages to escalate so much that we can no longer tolerate them. Remember Ellen's story, as she spoke of her denial and her inability to acknowledge her husband's infidelity? For her the "final straw" was the realization that for much of the time that she had been trying to "fix" her marriage, he had been having an affair.

Although it is usually the woman who files for divorce, sometimes it is the husband who makes the decision to end the marriage. He may do so by announcing that he wants a divorce, behaving in such a way that makes continuing the marriage impossible, or by simply walking out. If this happens suddenly, seemingly without warning, the effect on our self-esteem can be devastating, as Claire's experience illustrates:

"When he announced he wanted a divorce, I couldn't believe what I was hearing. There was never any question in my mind that we would stay together. We had had our fair share of problems, but divorce was never an option. I felt as though a ton of bricks had been dropped on me. I was absolutely numb."

Often when women like Claire come to understand the cycle of grieving, they realize that there *had* been many signs that their marriages were in trouble. Most often, their denial system had prevented them from facing this reality.

Regardless of the nature of the crisis, at some point most of us realize that we only have three choices:

1. To commit to and accept the relationship as it is.

2. To try to reconstruct the marriage with the cooperation of our spouse.

3. To proceed with divorce.

When we have finally run the course on options one and two, and when the consequences of *not* proceeding with divorce become too great, we will turn to option three. At this time we may become extremely depressed. We may develop severe headaches, intestinal problems, or other physical symptoms. We may believe we have finally reached the point of no return, only to relent and repeat the cycle of frustration. Each of us must ultimately decide for ourselves when to take step three in our own time.

There is short-lived relief that comes with finally deciding to proceed with divorce. However, the transition period that follows is long, difficult, and painful. It includes making decisions that will affect our lives for a very long time. Whether we are ready or not, we must face the practical matters surround-

ing our divorce. In the following pages, we will examine some
of the most pressing issues that we face.

Telling Our Family and Close Friends

Telling our family—our parents, siblings, and extended
family members—is one of the realities of divorce that is very
difficult. (There are many good books to help you approach the
subject with your children, so rather than go into that topic here,
I would refer you to the selected bibliography at the end of this
book.) Explaining a separation or divorce to family and friends
is often made more difficult by the fact that as Nice Women we
often shield our parents from our marital troubles because we
believe that we will be able to work them out and ultimately
avoid divorce. Consequently, by the time our divorce is inevitable, many problem situations have occurred over a long period
of time that have contributed to our decision to finally end our
marriage. It then becomes nearly impossible to try to replay all
of these problems to someone else who has not experienced them
and have them fully understand.

Another factor that makes telling our parents so painful is
that they are the primary source of our values on marriage and
family, and by divorcing, we are shattering their expectations as
well. The fact that many of our parents are still married only
magnifies their inability to understand the nature of our inner
conflict and the guilt that we feel. Because of their belief system
and traditional values, it is not unusual for parents to subject Nice
Women to harsh judgments and a long list of "shoulds" regarding
the "right" and "wrong" of divorce.

Our parents will often experience their own cycle of grieving
just as we have, with its stages of anger and blame, depression,
magical thinking, ambivilance, and bargaining. They may plead
with us to try once more to salvage our marriage. They may try
to get involved, to take over, to fix things. As much as most of

us would like to protect our parents from the hurt and disappointment that divorce entails, they will need to go through the process of grieving just as we have. Unfortunately, there is no simple way for them to get through the fact that their traditional values conflict with the reality of our divorce.

Our siblings and other extended family members will also react to our divorce in keeping with their own values regarding marriage and family. If judgmental messages were a strong part of our upbringing, we can expect that some family members will judge us also. The same is true for close friends. Many Nice Women find that some of the people that they considered to be supportive friends become cool and distant after they have gone through their divorces. It's not surprising that those family members and friends who have experienced their own divorces often provide the most understanding and support.

We are very fortunate if we have the support of family and friends during our decision to divorce and the difficult weeks and months that follow. I was fortunate to have support from my family—especially from my parents and my sisters. I have also been able to retain a few very special supportive friends throughout my first and second divorce. But I've also had to make new friends, and this has taken time. I now tend to seek out friendships with other women who have shared similar experiences. The mutual support that we give each other is invaluable. Even with this support, however, there have been many times since my divorce when I have felt very much alone and very isolated from family and close friends, especially during holidays. Unfortunately, this is one of the realities of divorce. Things never stay the same. We are continually forced to grow, to reach out and to experience the world in new and different ways.

Fortunately, in time most traditional parents and other family members find their own level of acceptance regarding our divorces, even though, like us, they wish there had been another option.

Legal Issues

It is very important that we take control of the legal aspects of our marriage's dissolution, because decisions are made during this phase that we will either have to live with or pay to change later. It is wise to educate yourself *before* you consult an attorney, because you will be billed for every minute of information he or she gives you that you could have learned yourself. Local libraries as well as law libraries have numerous books on the subject. Learn about no-fault laws, property settlements, and arranging for medical and dental insurance and college tuition. Become familiar with custody arrangements, child support, and visitation options. Take notes on your research and write down questions that you need to have clarified.

Even though do-it-yourself divorce services are available, most women seek the advice of an attorney. In choosing one, it is generally best to begin by getting a recommendation from someone you trust. If this isn't feasible, or you find you are not happy with the recommended lawyer, most counties have an Attorney's Referral Service that is listed in the white or commercial pages of your phone book. This service can provide you with the names of attorneys in your area that handle family law. The service can also tell you which attorneys are willing to provide half hour initial consultations for free or a reduced fee. Once you receive the names and phone numbers, it is up to you to schedule the interviews and to reconfirm the amount of the fee, if any, of the initial interview. I recommend interviewing at least three attorneys, but you may wish to meet with more depending on the responses that you get. Regardless of how many attorneys your choose to meet with, remember that *you* are the one who is doing the interviewing. Be prepared with a list of questions regarding your specific situation. Ask all the questions you need to ask until you get answers that satisfy you. An attorney who isn't interested in your questions, no matter how basic they may be, doesn't deserve your money.

Most attorneys require a retainer before they will agree to take your case. This is "up front" money to assure that he or she will receive payment for services rendered. Retainers can range from $250 to $5000, but no matter what figure you are given, don't be afraid to offer what you can reasonably afford. Retainers are often negotiable.

For most of us, legal fees present a problem. While the legal aspects of most marital dissolutions are actually very simple, every hour that someone spends on your case will be billed to you at an expensive hourly rate. Many traditional women have no money of their own, or perhaps the money they make is already committed to current bills and expenses. While some women already have lucrative careers or good paying jobs and have no trouble paying legal fees, they seem to be in the minority. Very few of the of the women I have interviewed for this book or who attend my workshops fall into this category. Because we have no other options, we often borrow money from our parents or friends, even though we have a very difficult time doing so. Or, we may sell our things to get enough money for a retainer. I sold wedding gifts, peddling them out of the trunk of my car. I had reached a point where I felt I had no other alternatives, and each time I sold something, I grieved—not for the material item, but because each sale reminded me that there was no turning back. At that point in my life, that was my reality.

Because the divorce process is so painful, there is a tendency to remain passive and to let someone else work out the details. However, there is no better remedy for the depression and feelings of helplessness that accompany divorce than to begin to take control of the important aspects of it.

When we don't get actively involved and remain weighted down by depression, it's very common to make decisions during this time that will be regretted later. Many of us have learned this the hard way, and it is especially likely to happen if there is another woman involved, or if other circumstances have taken a heavy toll on our self-confidence. So if you are in the process of divorce, take your time. Don't let anyone rush you; set your own pace. Become knowledgeable of the legal aspects of divorce *before* you make any long-term decisions on how to proceed. These choices are just the beginning of a whole new life of important decision-making.

Financial Realities

For most women, the financial realities of divorce are the most immediate and the most challenging. Many Nice Women have stayed in dysfunctional marriages because the financial consequences of separation seemed impossible. Unless there is a lot of money to go around, which there usually isn't, dividing a family financially can be devastating. Most states now have no-fault divorce laws, so no matter whose "fault" the divorce is, the financial split is fifty-fifty. If we're fortunate enough to have a lot of equity in our home, substantial savings and investments, and a minimum of bills, our financial situation after divorce may be tolerable. But often, money has already been a major problem in our marriages. With the continual escalation of the cost of living, few of us have large cash reserves or untouched equity. It has most likely been borrowed against for college costs, home improvements, or to pay off major expenses. We are generally not the savers our parents were, and with the relatively easy availability of credit, many of us may have been encouraged to live above our actual means.

As a result of these factors, divorce means starting over financially for most of us. It certainly has for me. By the time my divorce was final, there was nothing left. All of our resources had been used up on attorney's fees, business debts, back taxes, and paying off joint credit card bills and counseling fees. I always feared that I would end up with no money, even though we did have some equity in the house. The bills just kept coming out of nowhere, and by the time the decree was final, all of the money had been used up.

At the time that I was going through this, I felt so scared and alone, and at some inner level, I also felt a deep sense of shame. I somehow felt as if I was responsible for our situation, as if I somehow *should* have been able to prevent our financial devastation.

Since that time I have spoken to so many Nice Women who share similar stories. Some of them have been forced to file bankruptcy, go on welfare, or take other serious steps in order to survive. When we consider how divorce affects most of us financially, it is no wonder that the majority of single mothers live at or below the poverty level. Even though many of us have worked all our lives, we were not prepared to become financially independent. With this in mind, it's no surprise that among Nice Women, money worries are the biggest cause of fear, anxiety and denial when it comes to divorce.

In most cases, we are the custodial parents after divorce and are entitled to receive child support. However, most child support does not begin to make up for the income of another working adult, and only covers the bare essentials of raising children today. Also, in the case of a husband's second divorce, he may already be paying child support to another family. Unless he has a very stable, lucrative job, with lots of extra money to spread around, the child support for our children will be minimal.

Having a judge award child support is one thing; collecting is another. Statistics show that less than one third of noncustodial fathers pay child support on time. Even well-meaning dads can be late with payments, encounter job loss, or have a reduction in income. We have all heard, if not actually experienced, the horror stories about unpaid child support and unpaid bills. Even in states such as Minnesota that have excellent support collection services, a father must be behind three months before legal action can be taken. Then it may be two or three more months before collection is actually made, *if* there is actually money to be collected.

In my school-based counseling, I talk regularly with parents, many of whom are single mothers. Money woes—unpaid child support, not being able to make ends meet while working two jobs, and other financial problems are most often the the underlying factors which account for the stress in the family.

There is no doubt that divorce changes our economic status and financial expectations. We are not only faced with short-term decisions about how to survive day to day, but also long-range decisions about retirement. With these pressing concerns, it's not surprising that many women go from a first marriage to a second one rather quickly. The motives, whether conscious or unconscious, are often protection from the financial insecurity of being single or the frustrations of building a new career that will eventually lead to financial independence. Sometimes a second marriage which quickly follows a divorce works, but often it is only a temporary solution. Perhaps you can identify as I can with Sharon's story, as she tells of her experience with a second marriage:

> "I remarried in less than a year after my first marriage had ended. During that time I was receiving child support and maintenence, as well as working. I never really felt the financial strain, because within eight months I had remarried for what I later realized was the illusion of security. When that marriage ended thirteen years later, my family was in financial ruin. We had been living above our means with the help of credit cards. He had children from his first marriage, and so did I. We also had a child together. Now I was forty years old and still had no career that would support me as a single parent."

Many of us can relate to Sharon's story, since so many factors contribute to Nice Women being stranded without the means to be financially independent. Many of us elected to stay home to be with our small children, or we worked part-time in order to continue our primary role as wife and mother. Some of us dabbled in careers. We may have taught for a few years, stayed home when our children were young, and then given real estate or home-based sales a try in order to supplement the family income. In the meantime, the nation's economy changed, and the job market soared beyond our skills. When our divorces were finally inevitable, we blamed our spouse and the world for the predicament we found ourselves in.

As we have seen, anger and blame are a normal part of the cycle of grief which we all experience. We become incredibly angry because we don't have enough money, and feel guilty for having to leave our children in daycare. We blame our ex-spouses for the divorce and blame ourselves for not being able to find a quick solution. A part of us hopes to be rescued by someone or something. We were not prepared to be at this place at this time in our lives. Our traditional expectations were very, very different.

The reality is, of course, that there are no simple solutions to the financial dilemmas created by divorce. For most women raised in traditional homes, solving financial problems involves a complete restructuring of our notions about money, security, and being taken care of. There are emotional roadblocks such as fear and our innate dependency that keep us stuck. There are also practical roadblocks, such as the need to return to school or to train or retrain for the current job market. Meanwhile, there are bills to pay.

The only realistic solution is to begin to build a career path that will eventually lead to financial self-sufficiency. The process takes time, but it is the only long-term solution to the financial frustrations and realities that affect the vast majority of us. In succeeding chapters, we will explore how to begin that process in a manageable way.

Children, Divorce, and Single Parenting

Children are inescapably affected by divorce, but they don't have to be destroyed by it. Unfortunately, because of their own anguish, divorcing parents often unintentionally inflict severe pain on their children. In my work as a high school counselor, teenagers frequently come to me to talk about the painful feelings that continually haunt them because their divorced parents continue to fight, play power games, and blame each other for all their troubles. The divorce may have taken place a decade ago, but for these young people it seems like yesterday because the fighting, blaming, and guilt trips have never stopped. These teens are often depressed, and have been for a very long time. They often lack motivation, and their grades suffer. They may feel isolated and have difficulty with relationships. They may often feel guilty because their parents are so miserable, and at some level, they think they are responsible.

While this situation is much too common, it doesn't have to be this way. Our children aren't responsible for our marital failures, our financial frustrations, our fear, or our anger at our ex-spouse, and it's important that we let them know this.

Young children often feel responsible for their parents' divorce, thinking that if they had been better behaved, the absent parent might have stayed. Teenagers often experience conflicting feelings. On the one hand, they feel guilty because they think they should do more or contribute more financially, and on the other they are often angry because they don't have the things they want or feel they need. If we make subtle remarks such as "If your father hadn't..." or "If your father paid..." or "If he would spend more time..." we only intensify their conflict and the divided loyalty they feel toward their absent parent. Children deserve to grieve the divorce in their own way, but we must be careful not to unknowingly heap our negative feelings and frustrations on them.

I was determined that divorce would not destroy my children, and I developed a strategy so that the situation would not be any more difficult for them than it had to be. My daughter from my first marriage was seven when her father and I divorced. My son from my second marriage was six when his father and I finally ended a difficult twelve year marriage. In both cases, I made a pact with myself that I would *never* say anything negative or critical about either father in the presence of my son or daughter. Because the other parent is a part of that child, no matter how negligent that parent may be, any attack on the other parent is felt as an attack on the child. Sure, I ranted and raved and cried in private and among good friends and family, but never in front of my children. They were and still are the most important people in this world to me.

My daughter is now in her early twenties and recently graduated from college. Her father and I attended the graduation together. We reminisced about old times, about how young and naive we were when she was born. On her graduation day some twenty-two years later, our daughter looked so happy. She was so glad to have us both there, sitting together at the ceremomy. She told us later that it was the best graduation present we could ever have given her.

It wasn't easy getting to the point where I could do this. Over the years I bit my tongue many times when I could have lashed out. I helped her through the times when her father was not available to her because of his own problems. In short, I saved my adult judgments to share with other adults. Eventually, my daughter and her father found a relationship that worked for both of them. The bottom line is that she's a confident young woman who always knew she had permission to love both parents, no matter what our failures might have been. In turn, this gave her permission to love herself, because she is part of both of us.

Part of the difficulty of adapting to being a single parent is the fact that we have no role model. Most of us were raised in traditional homes where our father was the primary breadwinner and our mother was a homemaker who tended to the needs of her family. The chores were pretty much divided along masculine/feminine lines. Father took care of the car, the home maintenance, and the yard work. Mother managed the cooking, the cleaning, the laundry, and the children. It was a system that, for the most part, worked quite well.

Now, however, the traditional roles that we were raised with are no longer adequate. Becoming a single parent requires dramatic changes in our lives, and the pictures in our childhood albums do not fit the reality of our current demands. We can no longer devote all of our time to being a mother, tending to the care and nurturing needs of our children. We are now full-time single parents who most often must also work a full-time schedule. We are required to be a cook, chauffer, housekeeper, breadwinner, manager, and financial wizard. Our children still expect us to meet their emotional and physical needs, seemingly leaving us no time for our own. The role of a single parent is one that we weren't prepared for, and in most cases didn't want. As a result, many of us find ourselves on a treadmill of anger, blame, denial, and pervasive depression when faced with the burdens of our situation.

This mother's dilemma illustrates this quite well. As the parent of one the students I counsel, she came to talk to me about her son's failing grades, and told me of some of the circumstances in her life:

> "Since my divorce five years ago, our lives have been a disaster. I'm forced to work two jobs in order to make ends meet, and even then there's never enough money. I know I should supervise the kids' homework more, but

I work three nights a week, and they're on their own a lot. By the time I get home, I'm just too exhausted to follow through. In fact, I'm tired all the time. How can I *make* him do his homework, anyway? He says he wants to go to college, but right now he seems more interested in working part-time so he can buy the shoes and clothes that his friends have. His father is four months behind in his child support, and I can't afford to buy my son the expensive label clothes. Now I find out his grades are failing... Things were never this bad before his father and I were divorced."

The sad fact is that this mother's scenario is not unusual. Five years after her divorce, she was still a victim of it. She felt helpless—like a child waiting to be rescued. She had made no plans to carve out a career that would be more satisfying to her. By not setting limits on her son's behavior, such as demanding reasonable academic performance, she was unknowingly giving him permission to fail. She still blamed her ex-husband for her predicament. She was stuck in a cycle of victimization that many single mothers are caught in, with no plans for a better life.

Over and over again in my own life as a single parent, and in the lives of the many women who have contributed to this book, one driving question surfaces over and over again: *Why is the role of single parent so difficult?* After all, we are intelligent, capable women.

I've analyzed this question in my own life for years, and explored it in the lives of other Nice Women. The conclusion I have come to is this: *For all of the values it may have taught us, the traditional feminine socialization process does very little to provide us with the life skills and psychological stamina needed to undertake role of single parent.*

Although we don't always believe it, we do have choices. One choice is to stay stuck in a cycle of anger, blame, and depression. These emotions certainly feel familiar. The only problem with such a strategy is that it provides us with an excuse not to grow. As long as we feel that someone or something out there is responsible or to blame, we are hopelessly stuck. Only through real growth, which inevitably involves some pain, can we hope for a better life.

The challenge, if we are willing to accept it, involves the process of scrutinizing our feminine socialization process and the traditional expectations we were raised with. We must take an honest and often painful look at all the messages that have shaped us into the Nice Women we are today and sort out those that need to be modified. We may have to discard some messages and replace them with more productive ones. We don't want to stop being Nice Women, but we do want to be *capable* women who are in control of our lives, *even though the lives we are now faced with are not the lives we pictured.*

We need to take a hard look in our mirror and begin to internalize those images that are a product of the part of ourselves that is fiercely dedicated to growth. For it is only through growth that we can hope to reach the last stage of the grieving process—the stage of resolution.

In the next chapter we will reexamine the voices that shaped us, and develop a process for reevaluating the messages we still carry inside us in order to claim a *new voice* whose messages are more relevant to the demands of our current lives.

In the exercises that follow, you will be asked some thought-provoking questions. They are not meant to be answered quickly, or even necessarily at the first reading.

The questions on the grieving process are designed to help you identify what you have been feeling, and to understand that although the process of grieving a marriage is very painful, it is necessary in order to move on with our lives.

The questions on the realities of divorce are designed to

encourage you to think about the challenges that you are now facing and will continue to face for a long time to come.

EXERCISES FOR SELF-DISCOVERY

Assessing Our Grieving Process

Answer the following questions with respect to these stages of grief:

anger/blame	**magical thinking**
depression	**denial**
ambivalence	**bargaining**

In what stage or stages of the grieving process do you feel you have spent the most time?

Do you feel you are stuck in a stage or station of grieving right now? If so, which one?

In which stage do you feel you have spent the least amount of time?

What steps do you feel you can take or are taking towards resolution?

Confronting the Realities

Which legal issues have presented (or do you expect will present) the most difficulty?

What financial realities are going to require the most time and energy to resolve?

What aspects of the single parenting role are the most difficult for you?

What strategies have you developed (or are you trying to develop) in order to help your children cope with your divorce?

The questions in these exercises are ones that you may wish to come back to from time to time as you begin to develop your own strategies for growth.

Six

Claiming Our Own Voice

"Being stuck" and "feeling trapped" are phrases that Nice Women frequently use when they describe their lives in the pre-divorce, mid-divorce, and the post-divorce stages of what is a very difficult process. In a previous chapter, Rachel, who was facing a second divorce, described "trying every strategy she could think of" in order to save her marriage. She often became depressed when those strategies didn't work, but kept trying for years before her marriage officially ended. Bonnie, the mother of my high school student whose grades were falling, was still stuck in blame and anger five years after her divorce. Both women unconsciously were waiting for something magical to happen in order to be rescued from the frustrations of their situations.

In Rachel's case, she was bombarded by messages that admonished her for "letting" her marriage fail, as well as messages that affirmed her desire to please or to fix things and those which reinforced her innate sense of helplessness. The messages which guided Rachel may sound familiar to you:

"Endurance is the key to a happy marriage."

"I can make this work."

"Who will take care of me?"

"You should stick it out for the children's sake."

What keeps us stuck in self-defeating patterns that sap our energies, often for years? It is the constant replaying of our childhood messages, which may be negative or conflicting, blatant or subtle, but are always very powerful. If we are to become unstuck—to take control of our lives—we not only have to learn to tune in to our messages, but also to become skilled at analyzing them. This is not an easy process, because in doing so we may have to give up some beliefs and behaviors that we've become very accustomed to in our day to day lives.

Identifying Our "Stuck" Messages

There are several effective ways to tune in to the messages that limit us. The first is to become aware of our *emotional cues.* This process involves developing a sensitivity to how we are feeling and identifying the situations which are causing those feelings. Since our messages are often unconscious, we may experience them as a vague feeling rather than a clear directive. By learning to tune in to our emotional cues, we can begin to identify those messages that cause us to feel "stuck."

For example, I was determined to get my body back in shape after giving birth to my son. I was thirty-five at the time, and I set out to exercise more regularly than I ever had before. For years I had struggled to make exercise a priority, but my goal always seemed to elude me.

This time I was more determined than ever. However, as I had done so often before, I would find myself skipping exercise class more often than not because I felt I needed to do something else. Instead of exercising, I might run a special errand for a friend, clean up the kitchen, iron a cheerleading uniform for my daughter, or stay home with my tired son instead of bringing him to the nursery. There was always something that interfered with me getting back in shape. Each time I missed class, I felt frustrated and vaguely depressed. Too frequently I blamed my family for not "letting" me go to my class because of their demands.

What I didn't realize as I was doing this was that I was replaying a childhood message over and over again. That message was: "Always put the needs of others before your own." It was a message that I had complied with as a child. Now, as an adult, it was holding me back. I was angry, yet I felt powerless to do anything about it. That anger manifested itself as frustration and depression, as well as critical comments directed towards my family.

The way I denied myself my exercise class is a good example of the power of our early conditioning. I talk to women all the time who say that they *want* to exercise but don't because they just can't find the money, time, or energy. They explain that their children are too demanding, it's not worth the hassle of getting everyone in the car, or that they feel they can't spare the money. As I did, they let it slip down their list of priorities, yet they continue to hate the way they look and feel. They are stuck, just as I was.

I've now managed to make exercise a regular part of ny life, but not without a struggle. In order to modify my childhood message of meeting everyone's needs first, I had to learn to tune in to the emotional cues which accompanied that message. My repeated feelings of frustration and depression were my signals that it was an *internal* obstacle that caused me to deny my own needs, not the demands of my family.

It has taken me years to modify the message that not only

kept me from going to exercise class, but also from taking other important steps in my life. *I'm finally learning that my needs are as important as the needs of others, and that I can trust myself to make the appropriate choice.* It feels very, very good to acknowledge this.

Usually the emotional cues that accompany the messages which keep us "stuck" or in conflict are unpleasant ones, like my feelings of frustration and depression. Since Nice Women often deny their own unpleasant feelings, we need to become keenly aware of *when* and *why* we are feeling tired, angry, frustrated, guilty, or depressed. We need to become *self-oriented* in order to do this, which is also contrary to our early conditioning. The following emotional states are ones which a group of Nice Women from one of my workshops identified as those that accompany their feelings of being "stuck":

guilt	shame
blame	gullibility
incompetence	omnipotence
dependency	helplessness
frustration	fear
perfectionism	indecisiveness
insecurity	depression
powerlessness	resentment
passivity	denial

When we experience any of these feelings over a period of time, we need to examine the possibility that the feeling is an emotional cue generated from a replay of a childhood voice or message of a critical or limiting nature. To help us do this, we can ask ourselves a series of questions:

What emotion or emotions am I feeling? (Review the list of "stuck" feelings if you need help to identify them.)

Who or what in my current situation is causing me to feel this way?

What childhood message am I replaying?

Let's examine Valerie's situation to see how this process works. Look for the answers to the questions above as she shares her feelings about ending her twenty-two year marriage:

"Every time I faced the possibility of a getting a divorce I panicked. There was so much I didn't know. I didn't even know you needed a retainer to get a lawyer, or how much it would cost to live on my own. I knew nothing about custody arrangements or whether or not I would be able to keep our house. Each time I got close, I backed off. Even though the marriage was unlivable, at least I had the semblance of security: a home, husband, and children."

There are several emotional cues that emerge from Valerie's story which reflect her childhood conditioning. Her feelings of fear, dependency, and helplessness are evident as she describes her reluctance to give up the security of her unlivable marriage. Her childhood message probably sounds something like "females need to be taken care of and cannot make it on their own in a man's world." Each time she took a step towards ending her marriage, this message replayed, causing her feelings of fear, helplessness, and dependency to resurface. This typically traditional message actually *reinforced* her helpless behavior and discouraged her from taking steps towards independence.

Sometimes there are several messages involved. Going back to my exercise dilemma, you may spot other messages that stem from my traditional background. Consider the behaviors that kept me stuck. I felt that cleaning my kitchen took precedence over my desire to exercise. The message that was replaying in my subconscious was "Work comes before play." There were also hints of my perfectionistic messages. A tired child was very difficult for me to tolerate, even temporarily. A banana or a box of animal crackers would have probably appeased my son for an hour, but that wasn't okay with me. In other words, only if conditions were perfect could I give myself permission to do something for *me,* which in this case was exercise.

Another way to identify those messages that keep us stuck is to look for the presence of childhood coping strategies which often result in self-defeating behavior or "stuck" feelings. In Chapter Four, we learned that as Nice little girls, we often developed an overreliance on these coping strategies in order to gain acceptance from the important figures in our lives.

Because our patterns of overcompliance are automatic we must stay vigilant in order to detect their presence in our lives. For example, we may say "yes" to our child's request to have a friend sleep over when we really need a quiet, uneventful evening. We may say "yes" to volunteering for the school fair or little league committee when we are already overstressed and overextended. We may "agree" to conditions in our marriages which go against our needs or values in order to avoid conflict. We may also accept terms in our separation agreement which may not be financially realistic rather than risk appearing greedy or uncooperative. We may postpone making plans for a new career that will enable us to become financially self-sufficient because we are too busy complying with the needs of others.

We may habitually sulk, withdraw, or wallow in depression rather than modify the childhood coping strategies that keep us stuck. We may continue to caretake others while denying our own needs, partially because it "feels" right and partially because we don't really know what our own needs are.

Even when we are aware of one childhood coping behavior, we may fall back on another, such as manipulation, which we use to try to gain control of our lives. Also, our fear of failure—of not being perfect—will keep us from taking any important risks, such as going back to school or training for a new career. We tend to continue to do those things which we know well rather than develop the strategies that are necessary to complete long-term goals.

In order to get out of this rut, we must first learn to recognize those coping strategies and messages that keep us stuck. We must then learn to analyze and modify many of our childhood messages. Until we do, we will be a victim not only of our internal messages, but also of our divorce and the new demands it places on our lives.

Analyzing Our Messages

Getting "unstuck" always requires action. The problem is, we often don't know where to begin. By analyzing our messages, we can choose which ones are relevant to our current lives and which ones are archaic or self-defeating. Through a process of *rethinking, reasoning,* and *evaluating,* we can begin to develop our own voice. This *new voice* then becomes the core of our new self-image, one which exercises choice and is not a victim of any past conditioning which limits our potential.

This *new voice* will act like our own internal best friend. It will not judge us. It is calm, rational, caring, and patient. It won't accept self-defeating behaviors that keep us stuck. It will seek solutions and understand that change takes time.

Let's apply this *rethinking, reasoning,* and *evaluating* process to Rachel's messages from the beginning of the chapter. You will recall that her childhood messages reflected her fear of abandonment and of being alone. They also reinforced her desire to be taken care of, or rescued. By developing her *new voice,* she can analyze these messages and decide if her childhood fears and wishes are productive or self-defeating at this point in her life. After *rethinking, reasoning,* and *evaluating* her fear of abandonment, the input from her *new voice* might sound like this:

> "When I was a child it was appropriate for me to be afraid
> of being alone, but now I am an adult woman. Even
> though I may *feel* afraid, I will not allow my fears to
> control my life by keeping me "stuck." Many people feel
> afraid or lonely at times. In time, I will become more
> comfortable in my aloneness."

   It is important to recognize that our new voice *should*
always *acknowledge our childhood messages and the feelings
they evoke.* It does not deny their importance, but instead
provides rational, productive alternatives. This is how Rachel's
new voice might respond to her wish to be rescued:

> "It's true that part of me still wants to be rescued. It
> would make things so much easier. I wouldn't need to go
> back to school in order to get a better job so that I can
> work toward becoming financially independent.   I
> wouldn't have to confront my feelings of inadequacy, or
> my fears. But realistically, the only thing I can rely on to
> support me is me. I must take steps in order to become
> self-reliant and independent. Even though I feel afraid,
> the reality is that I've been very depressed in my depen-
> dency. It hasn't really worked for me anyway."

   Through the process of *rethinking, reasoning,* and *evaluating,* Rachel became free to examine options and alternatives she
had not considered previously. For example, she had always
equated being alone with being divorced or being without a
husband. This message was supported by her childhood conditioning. When her marriage finally ended, she was very much
alone.
   Like many women, she had neglected female friendships for

years in order to put all of her energy into "fixing" her marriage. By developing and utilizing her *new voice* after her divorce, she became aware of alternatives to the total aloneness that the child within her dreaded. Renewing and initiating female friendships was an excellent place to start.

By reasoning through her fears, Rachel opened up new options. Her thinking became less rigid, less black and white. She began to take steps to assume responsibility for her loneliness rather than continue to blame her failed marriage.

Each time we filter a message through this process, we strengthen our ability to do so with other messages. Each time we *rethink, reason,* and *evaluate* rather than automatically act or react, we begin to integrate our *new voice* into our personality. In essence, we are creating a *new self*—a self that is not merely a reflection of the past, but one that is real, spontaneous, and aware of what is happening now.

In developing this *new self,* we do not discard our past. We glean the very best of our traditional conditioning and integrate it with the realities of our present life. We will constantly be making new decisions about our capabilities which are not limited by criticism, stereotypes, or feelings of inadequacy. This process of redeciding involves three crucial steps:

First, we must reexamine our old beliefs. Because our early conditioning influences so many aspects of divorce, this reexamination process is continual and neverending. We become a "work in progress," constantly rethinking, evaluating, and questioning the messages that shaped us. There are *four early decision areas* that we need to scrutinize very carefully during this process of reexamination because they are so deeply affected by divorce. They are listed below, with the corresponding questions we need to ask ourselves for each:

1) Self-image: Who am I really? Spiritually, intellec-

tually, and emotionally?

2) Marriage and family: What were my role expectations as a wife? As a mother? How do I need to modify
them? What were my expectations of marriage?
Family?

3) Career aspirations: What were my messages regarding women having full-time careers? How do I modify
those expectations? How do I really feel about my
capabilities? What kinds of long-range plans do I need
to make?

4) Financial independence: What were my early messages about the "breadwinner" role? Am I secretly
hoping someone or something will rescue me? Do I
really feel capable of becoming financially self-sufficient?

This process of reexamining old beliefs (including early
decisions that we made about ourselves) may appear overwhelming, and in reality it *is* a relentless process. The best place
to begin is with an awareness that the road to becoming independent emotionally and financially is a long and challenging one.
But it is better to start down this path than to stay stuck in the past.
*In fact, self-growth is the only way to achieve a satisfying,
productive life, whether we are single, married, widowed, or
divorced.* Divorce is not what we would have chosen. However,
with hard work, we can use it as an effective catalyst for growth
and change.

As we reevaluate the early beliefs we have formed about
ourselves, we can heighten our awareness if we take the time to
record or write down our thoughts. This takes discipline because
it is a self-focused activity and goes against our early conditioning. However, it is a valuable tool if we can integrate it into our
day to day routine.

Using a small notebook or diary, we can begin to record a few thoughts each day about the early decision areas we just examined. At the top of four separate pages, list *Self-Image, Marriage and Family, Career Aspirations,* and *Financial Independence.* At whatever point in the day works for you, begin to write down any thoughts, messages, or feelings you may have about any of these four areas. Each time you record a message, ask yourself: "What is the source of this message? Is it keeping me stuck?" It's a good idea to date your entries, and to start a fresh page when you need to. Try to make it a regular activity, but don't worry if you miss a day or two. Remember, learning to focus on your *self* is a new behavior, and one which will take time to integrate into your routine.

Each time you record a thought, feeling, or message about one of the four early decision areas, however, you will strengthen your *new voice.* In addition, the more often you redecide an old belief or message, the more you will learn to trust the *new voice* you are developing.

The second step in the process of redeciding is sorting out our "shoulds" and "wants." You will recall that our "should list" is made up of behavioral expectations that were internalized when we were very young. These "shoulds" are often rooted in expectations of stereotyped feminine behavior, rigid sex roles in marriage and family, and other traditional beliefs. They are also influenced by the related critical or limiting messages we received as little girls.

The following workshop activity is always an enlightening one. In it, the participants brainstorm their "shoulds" surrounding divorce. Each woman offers as many responses as she can to the following question:

What do I feel I should or shouldn't have done regarding my marriage and/or divorce?

The most common responses, which reflect overadapted notions of compliance, accommodation, and control, may sound familiar:

"I should have been more fun."

"I should have been sexier."

"I shouldn't have been so focused on the children."

"I should have suspected the affair sooner."

"I should have contributed more financially."

"I should have seen his mid-life crisis coming."

"I shouldn't have complained so much about money."

"I should have stayed in better shape."

"I shouldn't have been so focused on my degree."

"I should have been more understanding."

I could fill an entire book with the "shoulds" Nice Women have contributed at my workshops. Often they share their "shoulds" sheepishly or with humor, realizing in retrospect how absurd they really were. Yet if we never put our "shoulds" in perspective, we will continue to accept the guilt and blame for a failed relationship, as if we alone had the power to control its outcome.

The second part of this activity requires the participants to develop a "want" list—that is, a list of the things that they *want* from themselves, their marriages, or their families. The first thing many women list is, "I want to save my marriage," or "I want to make my marriage work." The problem with this type of "want" is that it assumes we have the power to make this happen, and that if we don't, we have somehow failed.

In a legitimate "want" we assume responsibility only for

ourselves, and accept the limits of our power. For example, if we say, "I want a marriage based on trust, love, and mutual respect," we keep in mind that we are assuming responsibility only for our own role. In doing this we learn that those "wants" which will improve our lives require hard work, and that we cannot merely adapt ourselves or manipulate another person in order to achieve them.

Once their "wants" are qualified in this way, the women are asked to come up with a list of answers for the question: "What is it that I *really* want?" This usually proves to be a much more difficult task than composing a "should" list. After a considerable amount of time, thought, and animated discussion, some of the responses that Nice Women come up with frequently are:

"I want to become financially independent."

"I want to make the divorce as tolerable for my children as I can."

"I want to focus on improving my self-esteem."

"I want a healthy, trusting relationship."

"I want to stop feeling guilty about my divorce."

"I want to modify my traditional expectations so that they are relevant to my life now."

If you compare the "should" list to the "want" list, you will see some very clear differences. The "shoulds" are rooted in the past and are based on behavioral expectations and gender roles that we learned as a child. "Shoulds" also have an undertone of magical thinking. "Wants," on the other hand, are based on our current reality and require much more from us in terms of growth and change.

In order to achieve an important "want," such as wanting to improve our self-esteem or become financially independent, we have to be willing to undergo intensive reevaluation of ourselves and our socialization process.

Carrying out an important "want" requires focus, which is the third step of the redecision process. Divorce, or the possibility of it, changes the direction of our lives. Unless we choose to remain victimized by the realities of divorce, we need to take steps toward a better life, and these steps require *focus*.

One of the most difficult things for us to do as Nice Women is to sort out all of the demands that are placed on us in order to focus on those goals that will make a long-term difference in our lives. This is a difficult task in the best of circumstances. During the process of divorce and its inevitable aftermath of frustration, guilt, and depression, it is doubly difficult.

We don't get divorced in a vacuum. Whether we are ready for it or not, life goes on. There are bills to pay, houses to sell, cars to maintain, birthdays, holidays, ailing parents, needy children, demanding teenagers, and many other pressing concerns. It's no wonder that as Nice Women, we often spend the majority of our time maintaining or surviving, rather than focusing on, for example, the goal of financial self-sufficiency.

To focus on such a goal, we have to decide what it is we really need. We can start by seeking answers to the following questions:

What is it I really need, or need to do?

What is the most important thing for me to focus on?

What is the first step I need to take?

What do I need to spend my energy on in the next 6 weeks? 6 months? 12 months? 2 years?

Obviously, the answers to these questions do not come easily or quickly. Most often we need to spend time in careful self-assessment before we even begin to figure out what direction we should take. In the meantime, the day to day demands continue.

My own journey has been a slow, frustrating, and often difficult one. In 1983, when it seemed certain that my second marriage was not going to survive, I had to take a long, hard look at my ability to support myself. I also had to look at who I was and where I was going if my marriage did end. At the time, I still hoped that my husband and I could reconcile our differences and solve the problems in our marriage.

I was directing the Montessori School at the time, and although the school supported itself, it did not provide enough income for me to be financially self-sufficient. So even though I loved my work there and my staff, I began to make plans to sell. The process of finding a qualified buyer—both professionally and financially—took over a year. In the meantime, I renewed my state license for public school teaching, which had expired, and began exploring options for full-time teaching positions. My children were ages one and a half and fourteen, so I wanted to avoid a long commute if I possibly could.

What I learned was that there was no longer a market for my degree in Speech, Theatre, and Psychology. I needed either English or Social Studies certification in order to get a position in the surrounding area. I had spent some time in real estate, but I knew from experience that the lack of financial security and the uncertain hours would not accomodate me or my children. I felt stuck, and although I fought my feelings of helplessness and depression, they reared their ugly heads again and again. I greatly missed the school and the day to day support of my co-workers.

I considered going back to college to get certified in English so that I could teach. Even though teaching is not a lucrative career, the schedule did mesh well with my parenting responsibilities. What I learned after ordering catalogs and calling around to various colleges, however, was that getting additional certification would require many hours of schooling without significantly increasing my earning capacity. I finally made a decision to pursue a Master's degree in Counseling because of my long-held interest in psychology and human behavior. I had also done a great deal of problem solving and "counseling" with parents in my work at the preschool and had found it very rewarding.

That decision to go after a Master's degree was the beginning of a whole new phase of decision-making. I learned I had to take a standardized test, the Graduate Record Exam, in order to be admitted to a postgraduate program. I had to achieve a certain score in the areas of verbal and math ability. I bought a study guide for the exam and took a practice test. I only scored 200 in math, and I needed a 500. I hadn't had any occasion to use algebra for fifteen years, and hadn't looked at geometry since high school. I didn't have a clue as to how to relearn the math necessary to pass the exam.

After checking out several options, I enrolled in an independent study course in math which was held three mornings a week at a local community college. Fortunately, the college had just opened a campus daycare where my son could stay while I took my course work and practice tests. Daycare was a new and initially painful adjustment for both of us.

It took me six months of study to get my math scores to the required level, but my journey didn't end there. There was still the graduate school application process, actually taking the entrance exam, admissions interviews, and, of course, the problem of tuition. At each hurdle, and as I faced the many hurdles that followed, I struggled to keep my focus.

Each hurdle presented new problems that had to be solved, and because I was coping with chronic depression, the problems often seemed greater than they actually were. Also, because of the demands of my family, each new problem took twice or three times as long to solve as it otherwise would have. *But no matter how long it took to get there, I needed to keep moving toward my goal of financial self-sufficiency.* Even when it seemed that a marital reconciliation might take place, I knew I still needed to have that option. Past experience had taught me that.

Three years later I graduated with a Master's Degree in Counseling and began a full-time counseling position the following fall. It was never easy. It still isn't.

I share my journey with you because you too may be faced with the challenge of becoming financially independent. You may be considering completing high school through an adult education program, or returning to college to finish a degree. You may need to train for an entirely new career and not know where to begin. *Still, I can assure you from personal experience that no matter what your journey requires, it can happen if you keep focused on your goal.*

As I worked towards my goal, my children became more self-sufficient and less demanding. As my self-esteem improved, I was able to express more of my needs to them and they learned, for the most part, to respect them. My daughter, who is now in her early twenties, is very proud and supportive of my work. My son, who is eleven...well, he's a typical preadolescent. However, when his friends get especially heated over a video game, I have heard him say, "Hey, be quiet, you guys. My mom is writing." In his own way, he, too, is proud of me.

The Commitment Inventory

At a particularly frustrating time in my journey toward autonomy, I developed a tool for getting unstuck and staying focused. I remember the day I came up with the idea very well. I was sitting at my kitchen table, staring into space. I had been sitting there for well over an hour. It was six weeks before my

Master's Comprehensive Exams, and twelve weeks before I had to complete my course work in order to graduate. My husband and I had finally separated. It was not by my choice, but it had been inevitable.

The atmosphere in our home was tense. My daughter was acting out her anger through heightened adolescent rebellion. My son had regressed to a needy, whiny replay of the "terrible twos" in response to the tension in the house and his father's absence. Our lives seemed to be in shambles, and I was on overload—both physically and emotionally. I wanted to cry or crawl into bed, or both. I wanted someone to rescue me, but there was no one.

I needed to get a handle on all that was happening. I went to my son's room and got several large pieces of newsprint from his art supplies. I taped the sheets of paper together to form a large sign, approximately three feet by five feet, and I taped it to the kitchen wall. Then, with a large black marker, I began to draw columns. At the top of the first three columns, I put the names of the graduate courses I needed to finish. On the top of the next column, I put "Comprehensive Exams." On the fifth column, I wrote "Clinical Project," which was an internship I needed to complete in order to get my counseling certification. On the sixth, I wrote "Family," and on the seventh, "Divorce."

In each column, I listed everything I needed to do and wrote down approximate dates for completion and deadlines. I put the most important or timely items at the top and worked my way down. These items included everything from organizing an upcoming birthday party to a planning a study schedule for comprehensives to putting together my financial records for my attorney.

For two hours I worked on what I came to call my *Commitment Inventory*. As I did so, something wonderful began to happen. I felt less frustrated and depressed. I began to feel a sense of *control* that had been sorely missing just a few hours before.

In the days and weeks that followed, each time I completed a task I crossed the item off with a large red marker. Each day I examined the chart and chose which task was the most crucial without losing sight of any of the others that were also important. I was regaining control, and it felt good. I found I was more capable of balancing the day to day needs of my family and the long-range accomplishments that were necessary in order to make important changes in my life. Slowly but surely, the crossed off items grew while the remaining ones dwindled. I received my Master's degree on time, and although my divorce would not be final for another two years, I knew that this tool for gaining control enabled me to reach what had once seemed like an impossible goal.

I still use my Committment Inventory system in my personal life and in my counseling, only now I keep my lists on large white boards, one in my home and one in my office. I share it with my students to help them gain control of their schoolwork. I have shown it to my counseling colleagues and to women in my workshops. It continues to prove an excellent tool for maintaining day to day tasks while keeping focused on long-range goals.

Strengthening Our *New Voice*

The focus of this entire chapter has been *reassessment* and *self-assessment*. Each of us has the ability to *rethink, reason, and evaluate* our past conditioning. Each time we do so—each time we analyze our messages and identify our self-defeating behaviors—we strengthen our *new voice*, which is the core of our *new feminine self*. Once we begin to incorporate this process into our day to day lives, something very significant begins to happen. Almost without realizing it, we begin to look outside ourselves less and begin, very slowly at first, to trust what is inside of us more.

When we start the process, the rewards of redeciding are very subtle. In order to understand how it works, it may help to visualize your personality as a large group of muscles. Some of the individual "muscles" are stronger than others, but with use, any of the weak "muscles" can gain strength.

If we continue to use the "muscles" of our critical messages, they will remain strong. However, if we begin to scrutinize those messages and filter them through the redecision process, something else happens. Without continued use, our negative or limiting messages will begin to weaken or atrophy, and eventually lose their power. Then, the "muscles" of the messages that we strengthen and which make up our new voice will become stronger, and will eventually become dominant over the old ones.

As I've said before, it is not an easy process. Real change takes time, because we are integrating new behaviors into our personality. Change can also be very threatening, since we are often forced to realize that many of our familiar and comforting childhood beliefs regarding marriage and family simply don't hold true anymore now that we are face to face with the realities of divorce.

It is normal to experience a certain grieving for this loss, a loss felt most deeply by the little girl within us. It often helps to give that part of us permission to grieve, to feel angry, or to be depressed. These feelings of the child within are part of us, and shouldn't be ignored. We can soothe the little girl inside of us with a *new voice* that is patient, sympathetic, and based in reality. We must keep in mind, however, that there will always be a part of us that grieves the disappointments that divorce entails.

Another equally normal reaction to reevaluating and redeciding is our tendency to *overemphasize* the process in the beginning. We may become very focused on analyzing and filtering each message, and our minds may become preoccupied with this cognitive process. As a result, we may become somewhat *self-centered,* and this may feel unfamiliar. Family members may react either positively or negatively to this change. Instead of seeing this as a reason to abandon our efforts, however, we should keep in mind that this is a necessary part of the process. In time, the pendulum will swing back to a more balanced state. How long this takes varies with our own individual rate of growth.

In the next chapter we will explore how our *new voice* can be used to form the building blocks of autonomy, which are essential to the development of the *new feminine self.*

The exercises at the end of this chapter are designed to help you strengthen your *new voice.* Like most exercises in this book, they are not meant to be hurried or completed quickly. With consistent use, however, these strategies can become an intregral part of the *new self* you are developing.

EXERCISES FOR SELF-DISCOVERY

Our "Shoulds" vs. "Wants" List

Using a small notebook or diary, begin to keep track of your day to day "shoulds" and "wants." Divide a clean page into two columns. The left column is labeled "SHOULDS," the right column, "WANTS.

Each time a "should" message crosses your mind, whether it relates to your marriage, divorce, children, parenting, money, or some other concern, jot it down. And each time you are aware that you really "want" something, write it in the "want" column.

Once or twice a week, compare your lists. Ask yourself the following questions:

Which one is the longest?

Are your "shoulds" based on your past conditioning?

Are your "wants" things that you have influence over?

What messages or "shoulds" do you need to modify by filtering them through the redecision process?

What "wants" do you need to focus on first?

This activity may take several days, weeks, or even longer to complete. Take time to rethink, reason, and evaluate those "shoulds" that are rigid, judgmental or critical. Think about those "wants" or goals that are most essential to improving the quality of your life. You will want to include these goals as you design your own Committment Inventory in the next exercise.

Designing Your Own Commitment Inventory

Using whatever large sheets of paper you might have available, design your own Commitment Inventory. The only requirement is that it should be posted in an area that is easily visible to you at some point in your day.

Create a column for each area of responsibility in your life, as I did in my example earlier in the chapter. Yours may include family, community or church, your career aspirations, your commitment to take classes to complete a degree, or any other important goal you may have. (If you don't have a specific career goal, that column could be labeled "Long-Range Career Plan." In it, you could begin to list those questions for which you need to find answers.)

Under each column, list all the tasks, both large and small, that you need to accomplish, and include an approximate date or deadline for when they need to be done. Put the most pressing tasks at the top of the list and work down to those which you would like to accomplish at some yet undetermined time in the future. An example might look like this (although, of course, you are likely to have more than three categories and many more tasks listed under each one):

RETURN TO SCHOOL	FAMILY RESPONSIBILITIES	SEPARATION
take career assessment	arrange birthday party for Jeff	research child support
call schools for catalogs	visit with Elaine's teacher	interview lawyers
study catalogs	make list of chores for kids	
make appointment w/advisor		

Each time you complete a task, cross the item off your inventory using a different color of marker than you used to list the tasks. At times you may wish to add new columns, as circumstances require. *Remember, you are in control of which tasks you choose to do.* At regular intervals, make sure that you are steadily working on the long-range goals that you need to accomplish as well as your day to day responsibilities.

The Commitment Inventory is effective because it helps us to organize routine tasks and at the same time allows us to focus on those long-range goals that will improve the quality of our lives as well as our self-esteem. It also helps combat depression by providing a simple yet effective way to take control by sorting out all of the responsibilities that fall on our shoulders. However, like other strategies in this book, use of the Committment Inventory takes time and practice to become a permanent tool of our *new feminine self.*

Seven

The New Feminine Self

The ultimate goal of integrating our *new voice* into our personality is the attainment of autonomy. Being autonomous means being self-governing, making our own choices, taking responsibility for our actions and feelings, and throwing out limiting or negative patterns from the past. It does *not* mean that we no longer need other people in our lives or that we live in isolation. Nor does becoming more autonomous mean that we don't need healthy, satisfying relationships with others, including men.

Each of us has the capacity to obtain some measure of automomy in our lives. However, in order to achieve this we must "recover" three human characteristics that were an important part of our natural child. These characteristics are *awareness, spontaneity,* and *intimacy.* Those three words describe the vibrant, curious, and active little girl we once were before we adapted to the traditional ideal of feminine behavior.

By "recovering" these characteristics I mean that we may actually have to go back to the little girl in us to retrieve or release them, so they can help restore balance to our lives.

In the following pages we will discuss the three characteristics and examine ways to reclaim these essential parts of ourselves.

Awareness

Developing a sense of *awareness* means that we are sensitive to what is happening in our lives now. This kind of awareness is often referred to as "living in the here and now"—knowing where we are, what we are doing, and how we are feeling. As Nice Women facing divorce, all of our conflicting messages are made more confusing by the uncertainty of the future, so this is an enormous challenge.

One way we can strengthen our awareness is by becoming and remaining aware of our past conditioning and filtering old messages through our *new voice*. We can work to rid ourselves of rigid, archaic opinions that distort the realities of our current situation and keep us from accepting them. We can stop blaming ourselves, our ex-spouses, or our past conditioning for the frustrations of our current problems and concerns—whether they are proceeding with divorce, adjusting to single parenting, or deciding on a new career path.

Each day we can become more aware of how we continue to use our childhood coping strategies and fall victim to self-defeating behaviors. We can catch ourselves when we begin to revert to feelings of helplessness, inadequacy, or depression. We can make a conscious decision to take small steps towards autonomy rather than stay stuck and fantasize about being rescued.

We can also strengthen our awareness by sensitizing ourselves to our surroundings. We must give ourselves opportunities to revitalize all of our senses—sight, taste, smell, touch, and hearing—in order to regain and strengthen our capacity for awareness.

As a little girl, one of my favorite things to do was climb

trees—especially the apple trees in the orchard where I grew up. In the spring, when the bosssoms were full and fragrant, I would climb as high as I could and "hide" from the rest of the world. I had to sit very still so that I wouldn't annoy the bees that buzzed around me collecting pollen. I would smell the perfume-sweet blossoms and feel the soft spring breeze as it rustled through the branches. I would close my eyes and turn my face to the sky in order to feel the sunshine on my cheeks. I was not aware of my past or my future; only of the present.

We all need a place like that in our lives, where we can shut out the past and the future and just savor the beauty of the moment. Because it's difficult to reexperience the same solitary pleasures of childhood, we must create other ways to get in touch our senses on a daily basis. We can stop to imagine shapes in the clouds, or listen to the moaning of the winter wind. We can still feel the warmth of sun on our face, or walk barefoot in the cool spring grass. We can find pleasure in the aroma of fresh ground coffee or newly baked bread. Whatever we do, we can strengthen our awareness by striving to recapture the sensorial pleasures of our childhoods.

When we take the time to do this, we will spend less time thinking about the past and being obsessed about the future. We are able to *be* rather than *do*. While the process of strengthening our awareness takes time, for each new day that we engage in these behaviors we not only recapture a bit of the natural child within us, we strengthen our autonomy as well.

Spontaneity

For our purposes, *spontaneity* can be defined as the freedom to choose from a full range of behaviors rather than relying on familiar coping strategies or patterns learned in childhood. When we exercise it we have the option to choose from a wide spectrum of emotions and are not limited by feelings of inadequacy, helplessness, or dependency. We are not "locked in" to any feelings or behaviors, even the familiar ones. Becoming a more spontaneous person is very liberating.

Let's explore this characteristic further by reexamining the chart on page 64 and reviewing both the list of behaviors of the natural or uncensored child on the left and that of the overadapted child on the right. When we exercise spontaneity as an adult, we are free to choose an appropriate behavior or combination of behaviors, regardless of where they appear on these lists. In doing so we exercise our *new voice* and liberate ourselves from past conditioning.

When you first read this list of behaviors, you were asked to circle those behaviors you felt best described you. When you exercise spontaneity, you are no longer locked into those behaviors. You are free to choose from a wider, more flexible range.

For example, as I wrote this book, I had to be free to call upon the creativity and expressiveness of my inner child. However, creativity alone would get me nowhere. I had to also choose self-discipline in order to get my ideas on paper, which meant long hours at the word processor, editing and reediting. If I was too perfectionistic, the process would have taken forever. If I was was too self-censoring, I would have curtailed my expressiveness. If I was overly compliant in meeting the needs of the people that are important to me, I would never have finished a chapter. However, if I felt I was being too self-centered, I knew I would feel guilty.

By utilizing my *new voice,* I constantly made choices and balanced my needs and concerns. This enabled me to maintain a kind of flexible spontaneity. Of course, it took a great deal of time and practice as well as an effort to increase my tolerance for frustration to modify my old patterns of behavior.

As I became more spontaneous, I began to recapture the ability to decide for myself—my *new self.* My experience and those of the many Nice Women I have worked with prove that we can accept the fact that we each have our own personal history—our own repertoire of messages—but we are not at the mercy of them. We can become "the captains of our own fates," so to speak. As we integrate our *new voices,* we begin to steer our own ships. We realize that we are, within realistic limitations, responsible for our own destinies.

This new sense of responsibility requires us to make decisions that give positive and purposeful direction to our capabilities. We must not only make decisions that will positively influence our lives, we must *act* on them. Decisions without action will get us nowhere. In the next chapter we will examine some strategies for taking action.

Intimacy

As it relates to autonomy, *intimacy* means natural, candid behavior that is free of manipulative motives. It means that instead of always guarding or censoring ourselves, we become more willing to be open and honest with ourselves and with others. This doesn't mean that we inappropriately disclose personal information or "tell all" to anyone who will listen. We all know people who do this, and their behavior has probably made us uncomfortable. These individuals are letting their behavior come from their uncensored child, who doesn't know any better than to reveal personal or private matters in inappropriate settings. Still, there is a medium to be reached, and it is possible to experience a healthy form of intimacy with a male or female friend, a child, a parent, a spouse, or anyone else with whom we have a relationship. It simply means that we make a sincere effort to be honest, unguarded, and willing to reveal our true selves without fear of rejection. When we consider the socialization process we experienced as we grew up, it is understandable that most of us develop few intimate relationships.

The thing that most often curtails our capacity for intimacy and honest friendship is a poor sense of *self-worth*. If we don't know or like our *self*, it is unlikely we will reveal it to another person. Also, if we have revealed ourselves to another person in the past and been hurt or manipulated, we may be unwilling to risk doing so again.

Divorce almost always involves hurt and shattered trust, and it usually makes us fear risking our hearts again. At the same time, those of us who have been involved in a dysfunctional relationship for a long time often lose sight of what is honest behavior and what is manipulative.

Because of the emotional vulnerability that results from divorce and the pain surrounding it, it is often better for us to focus on our self-growth at first and to develop our capacity for intimacy gradually, in safer situations. A good place to start is by renewing old female friendships or by developing new ones with women who understand what we are going through. By going back to school or joining a support group, we will provide ourselves with more opportunities to practice our honesty and develop our capacity for intimacy. We will feel more confident in social situations as we strengthen our *new feminine self* through self-growth. As we do this, we find that we begin to feel much less vulnerable, and in time, more willing to take risks. Our self-confidence increases as well, as Beth's experiences illustrate:

> "Even before my divorce I never felt comfortable in social settings. I always held back from getting involved in conversations. I usually just listened and agreed with everyone else. I just felt safer that way.
>
> "When I started taking classes again, I was my usual cautious self. I didn't offer anything in class discussions and I prayed I wouldn't get called on for fear of sounding stupid. But now I have been in school for over two years and I'm close to getting my degree. It's funny, but I now

find that I am willing to risk much more and be myself. I am also much more honest with people face to face, and I'm not always so worried whether or not they agree with me or even like me. *I* like me!"

Changes in our self-image take time, and they do not happen without a conscious effort. But as we integrate our *new voice* and begin to make choices and decisions that lead to our improved self-esteem (as Beth did by choosing to go back to school), our capacity for intimacy improves.

Integrating the New Feminine Self

Through our expanded awareness we continually move toward a greater sense of autonomy. Each day our capacity for awareness, spontaneity, and intimacy grows. And each time we filter an old message through our *new voice,* or learn a new behavior, we become more *integrated.* Integration means uniting the very best qualities from our natural child with the wisdom of our *new voice.* We listen to our messages of encouragement and tune out those that are critical or limiting. We take responsibility for everything we feel, think, and believe. We stop blaming. We also realize that at times we may revert back to old behaviors, because there is no such thing as total or perfect integration.

As we use our *new voice,* we tend to become much more patient and generous with ourselves and others. While we realize that growth and change are frustrating and that accomplishing our goals may take more time than we had previously imagined, we develop the ability to deal with our feelings of impatience.

In accepting the fact that life is difficult and that financial independence requires work, planning and perserverance, we can transfer this same tolerance to those that we love and care about. In essence, we learn to understand and befriend our "old self" through the integration of our *new feminine self.*

The Behaviors of the New Feminine Self

The behaviors which are characteristic of our *new feminine self* usually fall somewhere between uncensored behavior and overadapted feminine behavior. The *new feminine self* adapts to each situation after undergoing the process of *rethinking, reasoning and evaluating*. In time, this process becomes integrated into our selves, and is automatic. The following chart illustrates the behavioral options of the *new feminine self* as compared to uncensored or overadapted behaviors.

UNCENSORED	OVERADAPTED	NEW FEMININE SELF
rebellious	overly compliant	adaptable
curious	uninquisitive	problem-solving
spontaneous	deliberate/controlled	natural
self-indulgent	always disciplined	self-disciplined
sensuous	avoids pleasure	enjoys life
fearful	gullible/naive	cautious/aware
aggressive	passive/avoids conflict	assertive
creative	self-censoring	focused/expressive
intimate	guarded/manipulative	honest/candid
self-centered	lacks self/caretaker	own identity/self

Of course, there are no rigid lines drawn between these behaviors; a behavior in the "uncensored" or "overadapted" columns may sometimes be appropriate. For example, we may "caretake" someone in a certain situation without losing our own identity, or choose to be guarded with someone when necessary without losing our sense of honesty. The difference is that our *new feminine self* has the flexibility to *choose* appropriate behavior, rather than remain stuck in old patterns. With practice, the newer, healthier, more productive behaviors become the familiar ones—the ones we are more comfortable with.

A key characteristic of our *new feminine self* is that it increases our power to choose and encourages us to constantly exercise this power. This is how the power of choice is demonstrated in the behaviors of the *new feminie self:*

> When we are *adaptable* we no longer automatically comply to situations. After thinking through all of our options, we then exercise choice.

> Approaching situations from a *problem-solving* perspective means that when we confront situations where we don't have immediate answers, we no longer revert to feelings of inadequacy or helplessness. We take the time to *rethink, reason, and evaluate.* We choose to find out what we need to know, and we are patient with ourselves in doing so.

> Our behavior becomes more *natural* as we gain confidence in our *new feminine self.* We choose to be less perfectionistic in our own behavior and develop a less controlling stance with other people in our lives.

> When we become *self-disciplined,* we decide what needs to be accomplished and what can wait. We adhere less and less to our "should" list and focus on accomplishing our "wants" more often.

> We *enjoy life* more by becoming more aware of the beauty in our daily lives. We choose to relish the small pleasures in our lives rather than focus on the negatives.

> Being *cautious and aware* rather than fearful in confronting the unknown lets us make educated decisions rather than gullible or naive choices.

> When we are more *assertive,* we can do what we need to do to get our own needs met without antagonizing or

manipulating others.

As we become more *focused* and *expressive* in utilizing our creativity, we don't flit from one project to another or censor ourselves when we have good ideas. We can trust our choices.

By developing appropriate choices for the expression of intimacy, we become more *honest* and *candid* in our day to day dealings with people, as well as in our relationships.

We are committed to developing our *own identity* by making decisions which will carve out and define our *new feminine self.*

Through this process of integrating our past conditioning with the flexible choices of the *new feminine self,* we are able to get in touch with and utilize our full potential. We often unlock capabilities that we never knew we had. Through integration, we are able to create, develop, and follow through on our long-range goals. We become "unstuck" from any past conditioning that limits us.

A big part of our past conditioning consists of the values with which we were raised. We may need to modify some of the values of our traditional upbringing in order to integrate them into our more flexible *new feminine self.*

We will face obstacles as a result of our divorce and its aftermath that we never thought we could overcome. But through the process of integration and by developing a *new feminine self,* we will have a much better chance of realizing our full potential and living a life that is satisfying, even if it's not the life we expected.

As we have discussed, changing old behaviors and establishing new ones takes time, conscious effort, and practice. Part of the reason is that in many cases, we are practicing behaviors for the first time—behaviors that even in the best of circumstances take time to feel comfortable. When faced with all the changes that divorce inflicts upon our lives, many of us must "catch up" and learn these new behaviors without the benefit of the normal, gradual developmental process of becoming independent.

Knowledge of our past conditioning helps, as does honest self-assessment. However, nothing replaces the fact that the process of achieving autonomy is a lifelong commitment for Nice Women. In the next chapter we will take a look at decision making and its role in the development of autonomy.

The following exercises are designed to help you practice autonomous behaviors. The first one is an exercise in *awareness*. It may be frustrating at first, because it directs you to focus on your self without actually "doing" anything. With practice, however, it will help you become more comfortable with enjoying a relaxed, meditative state. The second exercise challenges you to choose the behaviors of the *new feminine self* that you feel you need to strengthen, and make a conscious choice to practice them. By doing these exercises faithfully, you will be taking steps toward strengthening your *new feminine self*.

EXERCISES FOR SELF-DISCOVERY

An Exercise in the "Here and Now"

Experiencing the "here and now" can be a difficult challenge as our lives are turned upside down by the upheaval of divorce. Developing self-awareness is an important component to developing our autonomy.

Commit ten minutes a day to becoming self-aware. During this time, you are not allowed to think about the past or the future. You may want to designate a specific time or place in your day for this exercise, but the important thing is to work it in whenever and wherever you can.

Sit in a comfortable place—on the couch, in the grass, at the park—and let your concerns of that day float away. You can do this by concentrating on your breathing, relaxing your shoulders, and feeling the heaviness of your body.

Count backwards from 10 to 0 as many times as necessary to put worries out of your mind. Listen to, feel, and absorb the environment around you. You don't have to think; you don't have to work; you don't have to solve any problems. You don't have to *do* anything but sit and be *aware* of your *self*.

Practicing the Behaviors of the New Feminine Self

Review the behaviors of the *new feminine self* on pages 137-138. Which of these behaviors do you feel you need to practice the most? Write them down.

Choose one of these behaviors each week. Enter it on a page in your small notebook or journal. (Or you may want to add a new column to your Commitment Inventory and title it "Behaviors I Need to Practice." List the behaviors you want to practice in that column, with the most important one first. You decide what works best for you.)

Consciously focus on integrating that new behavior into your personality. Be aware that practice and frustration are part of this process. In time, you will notice that you are beginning to engage in some new behaviors automatically. Your tolerance for frustration will also increase. As these new behaviors become integrated, you will begin to experience a greater sense of automomy.

Eight

Decision Making: The Key
to Getting Unstuck

The attainment of autonomy is a process which requires the development and practice of such skills as decision making, risk taking, and self-assertion. Autonomy cannot be hurried or magically attained.

Psychologists have studied the development of autonomy for years in order to discover what factors influence its formation in both men and women. During the 1970s, a number of feminist scholars began to focus on the development of the female personality.

The research of developmental psychologist Lawrence Kohlberg received much of their attention, particularly his work on the differences in how men and women develop. Their study of Kohlberg's work revealed that the ego development of women is actually *slowed or arrested at an earlier stage than that of men.* Kohlberg's findings attribute this premature or arrested development to "...a nice girl orientation to approval and to pleasing and helping others; conformity to sterotypical images of role behavior..." Kohlberg's conclusions support the idea that our adherence to the traditional feminine stereotype of compliant behavior limits our potential.

On the other hand, according to Kohlberg, male development reaches a stage that is characterized by "...decision making, authoritative, achievement-oriented behavior." There are numerous studies which support this view of a more highly developed, autonomous male ego. Many Nice Women I've worked with agree that their upbringings reflect Kohlberg's findings on the differing personality development processes of men and women.

The bottom line for us as Nice Women is that we have more growing to do in order to attain autonomy. Since our traditional upbringings did not strongly support the autonomous behaviors of decision making, risk taking, and self-assertion, we must now learn and practice them until we integrate them into our *new feminine selves*. The process can be frustrating, time-consuming, and, very often, frightening. But if we know what to expect, we can arm ourselves against becoming discouraged and giving up.

Making Choices, Taking Action

One of the most essential aspects of autonomy is the skill of decision making. Decision making not only means making a choice; it also requires taking action. Without the ability to act on our ideas, we are forever stuck. The following questions posed by workshop participants who are facing divorce reflect the frustration and anxiety that we experience:

"How do I know that I am making the *right* decision?"

"If this is the *right* decision, why is it so painful?"

"What if I change my mind?"

"Where and how do I begin?"

These women weren't talking about what to fix for dinner or what wallpaper to select. They are facing difficult, life-changing decisions that affect not only them, but those around them. We all have the same doubts that they expressed, and the less experienced we are in making important decisions, the more intense our confusion and anxiety will be.

I can recall my own childhood experiences with decision making. When it came to the care of my siblings or carrying out domestic chores, I made many decisions daily, all in the realm of acceptable feminine behavior. I could plan a meal or delegate household chores with great efficiency, and I often received praise for my efforts. However, it was my brothers who ran the orchard business. They handled the money and made decisions regarding the orders. They negotiated with the grocers and delivered the apples that my sisters and I had helped pick, polish and bag. From my childhood perspective, they did the "important stuff."

When I had to decide whether or not to end my marriage, I was in complete confusion. Unconsciously, I waited to be rescued from this painful dilemma. At times I actually looked to my husband to rescue me, even though he was as stuck and confused in his own way as I was. This was the most important decision I had ever been faced with, and I had no confidence in my ability to make it and no idea how to go about it.

For Nice Women, the limiting nature of our traditional socialization has actually created barriers to decision making. However, if we recognize these barriers and understand them, we can reduce the power they exert over our decision making capabilities.

Barriers to Decision Making

As Nice Women raised in traditional families, our difficulties in making important decisions goes much deeper than confusion about which options to choose. *At the very heart of our dimemma is our confusion about our right to make important decisions in the first place.* The traditional expectations of compliance and obedience directly thwart our ability to think for ourselves, to make choices, and to act on our own ideas.

I observe this tendency in myself and in other women that I come in contact with on almost a daily basis. It is also very evident in my work with adolescent females who are grappling with career and college choices. Even when we have all the information needed to make an informed decision, we are reluctant to act on it, as if we are stricken with some vague paralysis.

The reason for this is that our internal anxiety creates increased pressure for us to make the *correct* choice. With each major decision, it's as if our *right* to decide is on trial. If we don't make the correct choice, we reinforce the notion that we didn't really have the right to make the decision in the first place. From my experience as a counselor, I think it's fair to say that while men may agonize over specific decisions, women also agonize over the *right* to decide.

This brings us to another barrier to learning to make decisions. Since we didn't have many opportunities to develop our decision making skills as we grew up, we lack confidence in our abilty to do so now. This *inhibited mastery orientation* is another obstacle which must be overcome.

As Nice Women, we have had lots of practice pleasing and taking care of others, and have been reinforced for doing so. Caretaking is second nature to us; we do it without thinking. However, when to comes to problem solving, weighing options, evaluating consequences, or acting on ideas that can have an important impact on our lives, we may feel helpless. Much of this feeling has to do to with the fact that our experience, or mastery orientation, has been limited. We haven't had very much practice.

If our marriages also followed traditional lines, we may have consciously or unconsciously deferred important decisions to our husbands, or delayed making them until we had his "approval." Until we make a conscious choice to develop our decision making skills, we will continue to be inhibited by our lack of confidence and, consequently, remain stuck.

Our capacity to tolerate frustration also plays an important role in developing decision making skills. Frustration is inherent in the decision making process and cannot be avoided. However, low self-esteem and a low tolerance for frustration go hand in hand. Therefore, if our self-esteem is low, or has taken a beating during the months and years leading up to our divorce, our tolerance for frustration will also be low. *This low tolerance for frustration creates yet another obstacle to developing decision making skills.*

Important decisions take time and most often require the gathering of a considerable amount of information. Those which surround divorce are rarely black or white, and are usually resolved somewhere in the gray areas of life. Also, such decisions often involve consequences over which we have little or no control. Both the difficulties of defining the options and the problems of dealing with inevitable consequences can cause a great deal of frustration. As a result, frustration tolerance is essential to developing decision making skills.

How then can we expect to make important decisions when we lack the tolerance for frustration which is so vital to the process? There are no "quick fix" answers to this question, but one way to improve our tolerance for frustration is to improve our self-esteem.

The only way to raise our self-esteem is through self-growth. By practicing the essential ingredients of autonomous behavior and becoming more skilled at integrating them into our lives, our self-concept will become stronger. We can methodically develop a *new feminine self* which is no longer a victim of circumstances, but which allows us to take control of our own lives. As our self-esteem grows, so will our tolerance for frustration.

Another barrier to decision making that Nice Women often encounter also lies in the roots of our traditional upbringings. As Nice little girls, we were often overprotected. Rather than being encouraged to "hang in there" when the going got tough or to face frightening or frustrating situations head on, many of our childhood messages reinforced rescuer fantasies and discouraged risk taking. We came to expect to be rescued from certain situations, and did not face and solve those dilemmas. This expectation is reflected in the experiences of the Nice Women throughout this book who grew up believing that "being taken care of," or "being protected from the harsh realities of life" was a kind of innate feminine right. We have all waited to be rescued at different times in our lives rather than take steps toward dissolving our marriages. Even after divorce, many of us continue to wait to be rescued from financial hardship or loneliness rather than take the difficult steps necessary to become more autonomous, self-sufficient human beings.

Another very powerful barrier to decision making is *procrastination.* The causes for procrastination are complex, and unique to each individual. However, what is often behind our procrastination is our need to have all the answers *before* we begin to act on our ideas. We want to know in advance precisely what will happen *if* we do this or that, and we become stuck in a quagmire of "what ifs." Just when we are about ready to take a step, a new "what if" pops up and causes us to delay. Here are some of the most common ones:

What if my children cannot accept the divorce?

What if my husband doesn't make the support payments?

What if he gets married again?

What if his new wife doesn't like the children?

What if I never have another relationship?

What if I can't find a better paying job?

All important decisions require that we risk some unknown consequences. Our inability to act without guarantees is directly related to our confidence in our ability to control our lives. If our lives have often been controlled by others or by situations over which we had little control, it becomes very frightening to accept responsibility for a life-changing decison that involves unanswered questions. Clinging to the "what ifs" gives us lots of time to stall and delay taking any action.

Divorce involves many unknowns. Even in the best of circumstances we have no guarantees that there will be smooth sailing ahead. However, as our sense of control and personal power increase, we become better prepared to handle "unknown" circumstances as they arise. We learn to accept that it is not possible to answer all of the "what ifs" in advance of making a decision.

Another factor that influences our tendency to procrastinate is fear. The process of divorce is a difficult maze that involves dead ends, pain, and seemingly endless anxiety. It can be messy, ambiguous, and traumatic. We don't know where the path will lead, and there is no one to provide us with the answers.

It is no wonder then, that it takes many Nice Women *years* to finally resolve an intolerable marriage. However, if we let fear control us, we are forever its victim. It is essential that we recognize our fear, confront it and deal with it. We can seek support from trusted friends and relatives, through counseling, and from support groups. We can also pursue areas of self-growth, such as career exploration, returning to school, or seeking a better paying job. The only thing that will diminish our fear is an increased sense of self-worth and power, which comes from our persistent commitment to self-growth.

Yet another contributor to procrastination is perfectionism, which is evident in *our tendency to wait for perfect conditions before we begin to take action.* We may fully realize that we need to go back to school, make a job change, or take steps toward dissolving a dysfunctional marriage. However, rather than begin the process, we wait for the "right" conditions.

We may feel we should wait until our children are older before exploring a new career. We may delay consulting an attorney because we lack enough money for a retainer. We may put off looking for another job until after we lose some weight or after we get over our current depression. In the meantime, we clean house or perform other familiar and routine tasks rather than explore unknown territory. We can find a hundred and one reasons not to get started, and so we wait for perfect conditons, as if they will somehow smooth the difficulties of implementing our plans.

However, the reality is that *there are no perfect conditions.* Perfectionism is a childhood perception; the real world is far from perfect. Of course, timing *is* important, and there may be a legitimate reason to delay taking action. It is when we are waiting for "just the right" conditions that our procrastination becomes another barrier to decision making.

It is important for us to be aware of these barriers which negatively affect our ability to make decisions. Like so many factors which influence the divorce process, our lack of decision making skills has been largely determined by our traditional socialization. Awareness, however, is half the battle. By recognizing and working on those things which keep us stuck, we can take steps to move forward rather than stay helplessly planted in our old behaviors.

The Process of Decision Making: One Step at a Time

Fortunately, decision making is a process rather than a giant leap. Important decisions take place over time, and involve the integration of five very clear steps. If we adhere carefully to the process and don't submit to the barriers just described, we can control much of the fear and anxiety that accompany any important decision.

1. *Knowing yourself* is the first step towards making a decision, and perhaps the one that is the most important to Nice Women. Because we were raised on traditional values which included traditional behavioral expectations, we need to reexamine and modify many of our ideas about ourselves, our capabilities, and our rights as women. We must often learn to think about ourselves in new ways which are more relevant to the realities of our present lives. This is not just a matter of knowing *who* we are, but also a matter of reexamining and reevaluating *what we can become.*

Perhaps the toughest thing we must reexamine is *our right to have needs of our own—needs that are equally as important as the needs of others, especially those that we care for and love.* Most of us were not raised with this belief. We often observed our own mother putting her needs behind everyone else's in the family. Many of us have done this automatically in our own lives for years. To be self-oriented was to be selfish. However, in order to get unstuck and to begin to make important decisions that will lead to self-sufficiency, we must begin to place *equal* importance on our own needs.

I recall a time in my life when I was struggling with a decision to go back to school in order to get my Master's degree in Counseling. This was an essential step if I was going to follow through with my divorce and ultimately become financially self-sufficient. I was confronting all of the barriers to decision-making, especially the "what ifs" and the right to have needs of my own.

I was consulting a therapist at the time to get some help sorting out my dilemma. My son was two years old—busy, demanding, and used to a great deal of attention from me. My daughter was fifteen—a cheerleader, active in sports, busy with her friends and often in need of a chauffeur. Although I didn't really enjoy housekeeping, I prided myself on the fact that I had a clean house, fluffy, fresh-smelling laundry, and served wholesome, home-cooked meals. My "what ifs" sounded like this:

"What if I can't continue to keep up my housekeeping?"

"What if my daughter needs a ride or something else that
I have been consistently providing?"

"What if my son doesn't adjust to having a new sitter?"

"What if I'm not there when they need me?"

My list went on and on. I remember my therapist listening intently. She took a long, deliberate pause. She then looked at me with direct eye contact and said firmly, "What about you? What about your needs? Are they not important also?"

I now understand what she meant much more than I did then. Attending to our own needs isn't an "either/or," "black/white" situation, which was my perspective at that time. *It is a matter of beginning to place as much importance on our own needs as those of anyone else.* It involves *rethinking, reasoning, and evaluating* old notions regarding feminine compliance. It requires modifying childhood messages such as "always take care of the other person's requests first" and "put your family's needs ahead of your own." Returning to school called for a reexamination of my own sense of self-worth, and of my early notions about feminine selflessness.

Stating that our own needs are important is easy. The hard part comes in *believing* that we have an undeniable right to our own needs and then *acting* on that belief. This involves making choices and pursuing goals that will lead to self-sufficiency, greater autonomy and ultimately, a *new feminine self*. It also means that at times those that rely on us will have to wait or be inconvenienced while we take care of our own needs. In the process, they, too will learn to become more self-sufficient.

There are many other traditional beliefs that we need to reexamine and reevaluate in order to know ourselves better. One that seems to affect all Nice Women is the belief that we are not capable of meeting new challenges. As the women I work with struggle to make decisions that lead to self-sufficiency, this theme almost always appears. The comments of Carol, Ann, Lois, and Ellen, participants in a career reevaluation workshop, reveal typically negative attitudes and doubts about their capabilities.

Carol, thirty-seven, is recently divorced. She has an undergraduate degree in Political Science which she has never used. She is currently struggling to support her two children by doing temporary secretarial work.

Ann is thirty-four and has completed some college course work but has not earned a degree. Before her divorce, she helped with her husband's business. She also ran a small but successful craft business from her home.

Lois and Ellen are both divorced and in their mid-forties. Neither of them have any formal schooling or training beyond high school.

Lois has been a homemaker, wife and mother for twenty years. Ellen has always worked, but was recently laid off from a middle management position that she had held for the past six years. Unable to find another job, she is now collecting unemployment benefits, but they do not provide enough income to meet the needs of her family.

The comments of these four women are typical of Nice Women who are at the same critical point in their lives:

Carol: "I've often thought about going to law school, but I'd never be able to pass the bar exam. Besides, I couldn't afford it."

Ann: "I'd like to start my own business, but I'm a real airhead when it comes to managing money."

Lois: "I've been a wife and mother for twenty years. I don't have any marketable skills."

Ellen: "It's been twenty years since I've been in school. I wasn't a very good student then, and I'm sure I wouldn't be any better after all this time."

These women are replaying childhood messages about their capabilities. They are afraid of not being "good enough," or of trying something new and risking failure. But when we don't reexamine our messages and modify them, we are stuck with our childhood insecurities.

An excellent way to learn more about ourselves is to make use of assessment instruments and career inventories. These tools can provide worthwhile feedback and concrete data about our personality type, our skills and abilities, our career interests, and our values. They can aid in our self-growth *and* our career decision making by providing invaluable information about our strengths, and can tell us how and why we would fit in a particular career path.

Most schools and universities, including community colleges, provide career counselors who can administer such inventories and help you understand what they show as your strengths. With their help, you will be able to make a more informed decision on a compatible career choice. Except for a small fee for the actual assessments, these services are often free. In other cases, they are usually available at a reasonable cost. There are women's support organizations such as Displaced Homemakers in many communities that offer these services on a sliding fee scale based on your income. Classes are also offered through many community education programs. If such opportunities for career assessment do not exist in your community, you can still do this on your own. There are many career-related books which can help you begin to develop an accurate self-profile.

While we need to know as much about ourselves as possible in order to make life decisions, we should not expect quick or drastic changes in our self-concept. Still, each time we learn more about our *self,* the stronger our *sense of self* will become. And our ability to make decisions will in turn be enhanced.

2. *Gathering reliable information* is another essential component of the decision making process. It is as important as self-knowledge, and often overlaps with it. Often our inabilility to decide results from the fact that we lack information. Take the four women that we heard from earlier. Each of them—Carol, Ann, Lois, and Ellen—made assumptions based on past experiences instead of facts. By gathering new information from reliable sources, they could modify their archaic beliefs about their capabilities.

For example, by writing or visiting several law schools, Carol could get information on tuition and entrance exams. She could also research statistics showing the percentage of female graduates. By talking to female lawyers and by visiting the local bar association, she could get a better idea of what a commitment to a law degree involves. She could gather information about other women's experiences with the bar exam, get an idea of an attorney's starting salary, and find out about working conditions for women in law. This information, coupled with data gathered through the process of self-assessment, would bring her a step closer to making an informed decision.

Ann, who wants to run her own business, can take a class or workshop on this subject in order to become more knowledgeable. She can meet with small business owners and organizations to ask questions about all facets of the process of establishing a business. She can inquire about and attend money management workshops for small businesses. The career assessment process will help her see if she possesses the personality and abilities of a successful entrepreneur. She can find out how much capital she will need, and if she is eligible for a small business loan. She has much to learn before she is ready to make a decision, but one thing is certain: she should not limit herself simply because she has always thought of herself as an "airhead" when it comes to managing money.

Since Lois is unsure of her skills, she needs to spend a significant amount of time gathering information, particularly about herself. She could meet with a career counselor and arrange to take a series of career inventories. She may benefit most from someone who specializes in reentry counseling, a specialized approach for adults in transition.

What she will discover is that even though she does not have experience in the business world, she does have skills, abilities, and interests that will *translate* to those needed in a suitable job. Many of the skills required to manage a family or run a household are the same skills called for in a variety of careers.

What Ellen, who is thinking of going back to school, didn't know is that *most adult learners feel inadequate at the thought of returning to school.* If she gets some reentry counseling, she will learn that contrary to her beliefs about her anticipated performance, adult learners usually *excel* in their studies regardless of how they have performed in school as a child or as a teenager. This is because adult learners are not only more motivated, they also bring with them valuable life experiences that many younger students don't have. These two factors often give adult learners an edge.

If she is very unsure of her academic skills, she can take a variety of academic placement tests to determine her strengths and weaknesses. If necessary, she can take a preparatory course or two to improve her skills before she decides to pursue a specific course of study. These options are available at most community colleges and adult reentry programs.

No matter where she starts, Ellen doesn't have to remain stuck simply because she doesn't have confidence in her skills.

Information gathering is important not only because it is essential to the decision making process, but also because it requires that we *assert* ourselves in order to find out what we need to know. This process of self-assertion contributes to the formation of our more autonomous *new feminine self.*

However, this is often where many Nice Women fall short. Because we are so competent in the realm of motherhood and family-related tasks, we find it hard to admit that there is so much that we don't know about the world of work and our ability to find a satisfying career within that world.

This is particularly difficult for us if we have perfectionistic tendencies. Somehow we think we *should* know what to do without going through all the frustrating hoops. But in order to call upon and benefit from the expertise of others, we must first admit that we are not "perfect" and that we have much to learn.

Even then, the information gathering process can be frustrating. Often it involves trips to the library, phone calls to individuals, visits to campuses, informational interviews, arranging for child care, and less time to take care of routine activities.

Frustration is a common cause of a breakdown in the decision making process. We can lose our focus and allow other, more managable tasks to become obstacles. It seems much easier to focus on those things that are familiar than to push on through the maze of information gathering. When we find ourselves falling into this trap, it is essential to remember that all important decisions involve some degree of conflict and frustration, and to consider the alternative of remaining stuck.

3. The third phase of decision making involves *defining and examining the options that now exist.* This occurs once we have gathered the information that we need. *The more viable options that we have, the less anxiety we will experience.* We may all be able to learn something from examining the options of Meredith, a single working mother who defined her alternatives after a series of career decision making workshops.

Meredith's long-term goal was to become financially self-sufficient. She had previously earned two years of college credit towards a liberal arts degree. She was working as a data processor, but was not earning enough money to support herself and her two children comfortably.

After months of self-assessment and information gathering she examined her options by asking herself "What realistic choices now exist?" She identified the following options:

a) To go back to college part-time or full-time in order to complete her Bachelor's degree in Psychology.

b) To get additional training within the company she now works for in hopes of upgrading her position and her pay.

c) To go to a private business school in order to earn a specialized degree in an area of the business world that has a promising outlook in employability and salary.

Through the process of self-assessment, Meredith gained knowledge of her skills and abilities. By accessing current data base information at a local community college, she learned the salary structure and outlook for a variety of careers which fit her own personal profile.

She knew approximately how long it would take to reach any

one of these three options, depending on whether she went to school full or part-time. She had also explored the costs involved in tuition and child care, as well as what financial aid options were available.

Because Meredith is a single, full-time, working mother, the process of acquiring all of this information took months. At times she became understandably frustrated because there were no easy solutions to her own personal needs. But the alternative was to remain stuck, with no chance to improve her life.

As we've discussed, our options are rarely black or white. In Meredith's case, she chose to pursue two of hers at the same time. First, she decided to begin work on a professional business degree in the personnel field, because the career assessments that she took indicated she had strong organizational, managerial, and social skills. However, because of financial and time restraints, she was forced to pursue this course of action part-time while continuing to work full-time. She also decided to take advantage of any training that she could get through her present employer. Even if she never got a promotion or a raise as a result, she would still gain valuable experience that would benefit her in any area of the business world. And if getting her degree took longer than she'd planned, she would have upgraded her chances for a promotion at her present job.

By researching her options, knowing her abilities, and acting on the information she had gathered, Meredith took control of her life and started taking the steps necessary to reach her goal of financial self-sufficiency. She was able to arrive at her decision with less fear and a greater degree of confidence because she had spent considerable time in steps one and two—learning about herself and gathering information.

4. *Weighing consequences* is the fourth phase of the decision masking process. This phase is very helpful in answering all of the "what ifs" that creep into our minds just as we are getting

ready to take action on the options we've defined. Weighing consequences provides a method for evaluating the reversibility or irreversibility of short and long-term decisions.

Let's return to Meredith's situation. She has made an informed choice regarding her options. She is in control of the path she has decided to take, and is pursuing two options, which serves to reduce her anxiety. However, there are still a number of "what ifs" that remain out of her control:

• What if she finds that the business course is not what she expected?

• What if she finds it too difficult to take the business course, work full-time, train at her current job, and have time for her children and herself?

• What if she is offered a better position with more responsibilities at her current job, and is pressured to accept it?

• What if she can't find a better paying job upon completing the personnel training course?

• What if she lands a job in personnel that requires that she relocate? How could she take her children away from living close to their father?

All decisions involve consequences, and because the consequences of our decisions are often unknown, we need to be aware of the fact that we cannot and should not try to anticipate every possible consequence or outcome. However, we can keep in mind that we *do* have control over how we choose to deal with outcomes. In Meredith's case, she can choose how she will deal with any of the consequences that may result from acting on her options.

She may even ultimately decide to reverse her decision to

work towards a career in personnel. However, if she let that possibility persuade her not to begin a path to change, she would assure herself of never reaching her goal of financial self-sufficiency.

Realistically, we should *expect* consequences and outcomes that are out of our control, and deal with them as they arise. This is certainly true in the case of the divorce process. However, the process will provoke less anxiety if we are aware of the aspects of the decision which are within our control. Whether we are deciding to divorce, to stay married, to get a better paying job, or choose a new career path, the process outlined in steps one through four is the same.

5. *Testing reality* is the fifth step of the decision making process. It is the step in which we commit ourselves to taking action—even if the action we take is in small, calculated steps. If we have done a thorough job with steps one through four up to this point, we will have reduced the fear and anxiety that often accompany decision making. However, because it takes time and practice to become more comfortable with making important, life-changing decisions, and because of the barriers that many Nice Women experience, we often must move ahead in spite of our fear.

We accomplish this with the help of our *new voice,* pushing through our fears in order to take action. In doing so, we recognize that our fears are founded on our old messages, and put them in the proper perspective. Our *new feminine self,* not our limiting messages, takes control.

In order to see how the testing reality or taking action step works, let's revisit the decisions that Carol, Ann, Lois, and Ellen are facing. After each woman has spent considerable time in steps one through four, they are now ready to test reality.

Carol has almost decided to pursue a degree in law. Her primary concern is whether she can handle the course work, her current job, and her family responsibilities. Rather than apply to law school at this time, she has decided to take an introductory law course at a local university through an adult continuing education program. By starting slow, she reduces her risks; she can test the reality of her fears. By taking this action, she will gain confidence in her capabilities, as well as in her ability to take the next step in her decision.

Ann has decided to take a twelve-week course at a local technical college titled "Starting Your Own Business." She still has concerns as to whether or not she will be able to support herself if she pursues her dream. She also lacks confidence in her ability to manage money effectively. By taking this course, however, she will strengthen her *new feminine self* simply because she chose a course of action rather than remaining stuck.

Anytime we make an informed decision, we strenghten the *new feminine self* we are developing. So even if Ann ultimately decides not to start her own business, she still has learned much and gained much confidence through the process of reaching that decision. Because she is developing decision making skills, the next decision that she faces will be made easier by the fact that she has been through the process.

After spending several weeks in valuable career assessment at her local community college, Lois has decided to pursue a job in retail sales. She has learned that she *does* have many skills and abilities that translate to sales work, even though she has not been employed outside her home for twenty years. She worked with a reentry counselor in order to develop her resume. Instead of listing "past positions held," her resume focuses on the "demonstrated skills" that she has been using and developing over the years, especially those that are often referred to as "people skills." She also attended a workshop that helped her hone her interviewing skills and roleplay a typical interview situation.

Her next action step is to conduct several informational interviews with major retailers in her area. By doing so she will get a feel for the job market and begin to develop a network of contacts. For Lois, this step still involves some fear and anxiety, but she has come a long way from the woman who said, "I don't have any marketable skills."

Ellen, still unsure of her ability to survive in an academic environment, has decided to commit to a full series of assessments, both career related and academic, in order to better define her options. Her goal, like many other divorced women, is to have a real career with benefits that will adequately support her and her children. The process of assessment will take her several months because of the demands of her current job-hunting and her family.

She has also decided that once all of the results are in and she has had a chance to discuss her strengths and weaknesses with a career counselor, she will then choose her next step in reaching her goal. She may discover that she is best suited for a more technical career, with less emphasis on "book" learning. By taking the steps necessary to learn about herself and her career path options, she has begun to test reality. In the process, she too is strengthening her *new feminine self.*

The process of making important decisions cannot be rushed. There are no shortcuts or quick answers. Each phase of this process: understanding ourselves, gathering information, examining options, weighing consequences, and testing reality takes time, patience, and an understanding that frustration is an inherent part of the process. It is also important to understand that the process of decision making is cyclic—that is we may need to recycle through the process more than once before we make a life-changing decision. However, if we commit ourselves to seeing our important decisions through each stage, we will not only begin to make informed choices, but will also strengthen our decision making skills and our self-image as well.

In the next chapter we will take a close look at self-assertion, another essential building block of autonomy, and learn why it is a vital part of our *new feminine self.*

The exercise at the end of this chapter is the composition of a worksheet to assist you in making important decisions. It summarizes the five steps involved in the process and provides a practical way to work through the steps and stay focused.

EXERCISES FOR SELF-DISCOVERY

The Decision Making Worksheet

The Decision Making Worksheet is a tool much like the Commitment Inventory. It is simply a way to gain a sense of control over the frustrating process of making an important decision. You can write out your Decision Making Worksheet on a single piece of looseleaf paper, or make it larger and put it up next to your Commitment Inventory.

At the top of your paper, write: "Decision I am now facing:" and put down an issue with which you are concerned. This could be anything from whether or not to begin divorce proceedings to how to explore a new career path. It might be a decision of whether or not to go back to court to change a stipulation in your divorce agreement, or whether to take steps to collect unpaid child support. It could also be something less weighty which is still problematic, such as being unsure of how to spend your vacation days.

Divide the sheet into five columns. Each column corresponds to a step in the decision making process. Label them as follows:

1) **Self-assessment** 2) **Information Gathering** 3) **Examining Options**
4) **Weighing Consequences** 5) **Testing Reality**

Begin with step one. This is where you will need to spend the most time at first. The question you are trying to answer is: *What do I really need to know about myself in order to make this decision?* Reviewing Chapter Six will be helpful, particularly the sections on the Four Early Decision Areas, our "Shoulds" and "Wants," and the importance of keeping our focus. You may wish to review other *Exercises For Self-Discovery* as well as any journal entries you have made. Going through the process of career assessment also helps you to clarify your skills, abilities, and values. These are the tools which will help you decide what it is that you need to know about yourself.

Under step two, list all the informational things you need to know in order to proceed with the decision making process. These could be in the form of questions, such as:

How much training will I need for a new career?

How much child support am I entitled to?

How much money will it take to live on my own?

Your task in step two is to find the answers to your questions. Remember that this step may be time-consuming and frustrating.

Under step three, write out all of the options you feel are possible after studying the information you have gathered in steps one and two. Your options are the different ways in which you could possibly meet your goal. Be sure to use the resources that have been suggested, and don't be afraid to seek help with this step or with the previous ones.

Under step four you will actually write out all of the possible consequences that might happen if you act on your options. These will be the answers to such questions as:

What might happen, positively or negatively, if I decide to proceed with my divorce?

What might happen, positively or negatively, if I proceed with my plans to train for a new career?

Remember, it is not possible to control all of the consequences. However, you do have control over how you *deal* with them.

Step five is when you begin to take steps toward reaching the goal which is the end result of your decision. Write out the steps you need to take, starting with the first one. You may begin by interviewing several attorneys in order to proceed with your divorce, or by taking a class in order to test out your ability to pursue a long-range career goal. Step five is where your push through your fear with the help of your *new voice.*

Don't try to complete your worksheet too quickly. Review each step in this chapter as often as necessary. It may take time to find out what needs to go in each column; making a commitment to begin the process is the first step. Remember that the first few times you go through the process, it will be frustrating and time-consuming. With practice, however, it will get easier, and over time the decision making process will become integrated into your *new feminine self.*

Nine

Self-Assertion: Much More Than Speaking Up

Self-assertion is an essential building block in the process of achieving autonomy. However, when we think of the term "assertive," different images come to mind for each of us. I often ask for definitions from the women in my workshops, and the answers I get reveal a variety of impressions:

"Assertiveness means to speak up."

"Being assertive means you don't let other people walk all over you."

"Asserting yourself means saying 'no.'"

While these answers provide some insights into assertive behavior, they do not begin to capture the full scope of what it means in the context of the *new feminine self*. In this context, self-assertion means strengthening and developing our *new voice* —the voice that we develop by evaluating our old messages and replacing them with messages that promote our self-growth.

Much like the process of decision making, self-assertion always requires taking action. And like decision making, it often causes us to experience many of the same fears and feelings of inadequacy. As we begin to assert our *new voice,* however, those feelings and fears will fade.

Nice Women and Assertiveness Skills Development

There are several areas in which Nice Women typically lack the assertiveness skills which are essential to developing the *new voice* which is the foundation for the *new feminine self.* As we examine these areas, we need to keep in mind how they contradict many of our childhood messages as well as many of our childhood coping strategies. Understanding this is the key to developing more effective behaviors.

Asking for what we need and going after it and following through until we get results is at the core of asserting our *new feminine self.* This skill is the opposite of our childhood patterns of overcompliance. It is also contrary to our patterns of self-denial, because in order to ask for or pursue what we need and get results, we first have to believe that we are worthy of the investment of time, energy, and perseverance that such action requires.

We also have to be willing to challenge the answers that we get along the way in pursuit of getting our needs met. It is often my experience and the experience of other Nice Women that when we ask for something, whether it is related to our divorce proceedings, our financial situation, our career exploration, or our search for a new job, we often get pat answers or answers that are less than satisfying. Our tendency as Nice Women is to accept these standard answers rather than ask again until we have answers that we can fully accept, or at least fully understand.

We don't need to resort to manipulation or revert to a show of helplessness in order to get the answers that we need. By utilizing our *new voice,* we can simply and directly confront the situation by asking a series of non-threatening questions, or make statements which will clarify the problem:

> "I don't think we are communicating. Would you mind explaining that again?"

> "I hear what you are saying, but the answers are not satisfactory to me. Let's see where we can compromise."

> "I understand that is your company policy. What I am asking for is some individual consideration to my financial dilemma. Let me explain further."

> "I'm not clear what my financial rights are in my divorce. I need for you to go over that again."

> "I've written down the answers you have given me. I will call you back in a day or two, after I have had a chance to think this over."

Each response reflects a position of self-assertion in the form of an "I" statement, rather than a position of overcompliance. If we take the time to *rethink, reason, and evaluate* the process of getting what we need, we are much less likely to get "stuck" or resort to the rescuer fantasies of our childhoods.

The ability to say "no" without guilt is another essential skill of self-assertion. As Nice Women, our natural tendency is to say "yes," to agree, or to comply, so the acquisition of this skill is especially challenging.

One way to counteract our tendency to say "yes" when we really mean "no" is to avoid hasty agreement to a situation without giving ourselves time to *rethink, reason, and evaluate* how the request or situation will affect our emotional and/or physical energies. Since separation and divorce present us with so many new situations for which we are not prepared, it is especially important that we give ourselves as much time as we need to process each new situation that comes along.

In Nice Woman workshops on developing assertiveness skills, participants work in small groups formulating creative yet assertive responses to a variety of situations. Their responses cover a wide range of circumstances, including requests from family members, children, co-workers, school officials, community and church organizations, and from ex-spouses:

> "Thank you for asking me to help. Let me reevaluate my present commitments and give you a call tomorrow."

> "Thank you for thinking of me, but no. I'm not able to take on any additional commitments at this time."

> "I'll need some time to think this situation over. I'll give you my response in a few days.

> "No. You can't have a friend sleep over tonight. Let's make plans for a date in the very near future."

> "Having everyone to our house for Christmas isn't feasible this year. We'll have to examine other alternatives."

If our habitual pattern has been to take care of the needs of others, saying "no" feels awkward at first, and feeling guilty seems to go with the territory. For a time, it seems, we must tolerate our guilt, and recognize it for what it is—the objection of the Nice little girl within us who feels she should always meet the needs of everyone else. It's that same little girl who doesn't feel that she has the right to say "no." However, as we strengthen our *new voice* and our *new feminine self,* we will become less dominated by our "should" list. As this transition occurs, we will find that guilt plays less and less of a role in our lives.

Of course, we can still do for others what we choose to do and what we can realistically manage. The difference is that we are now making choices after filtering their requests through our *new voice.* With practice, we can learn to say "no" or "not now" and feel good about the choices we have made.

The ability to be assertive without apology or self-criticism is another skill that Nice Women find difficult. If we listen carefully to ourselves and to other Nice Women, we will discover that many of us habitually sell ourselves short by discrediting, minimizing, belittling, and devaluing our own abilities and accomplishments. Perhaps these phrases sound familiar to you:

"This will probably sound stupid, but..."

"I was really lucky to have gotten that job."

"It's not perfect, but..."

"It really wasn't that good."

"I just happened to be in the right place at the right time."

In my day to day life, whether I'm in a work setting, among friends, at exercise class, in the grocery store, or any one of a variety of other places, I am tuned in to the fact that women constantly belittle themselves.

An interesting facet of this tendency to belittle or minimize ourselves is the fact that many of us who do this are accomplished, competent women who are utilizing our skills in a variety of positive ways. However, when we are discussing our accomplishments, we say things like "Oh, it was nothing," or "It wasn't that hard to do," or "It could have been better." Even when we are constantly offered realistic evidence that our capabilities are respected by others, we tend to dismiss the idea that it was our *competence* that has earned this respect.

What is the origin of such minimizing behavior? Could it be simple modesty? This is unlikely, considering the abundance of limiting or critical messages listed in Chapter Three that are significant influences in the traditional feminine socialization process. These messages downplayed our competencies, thwarted the development of certain abilities, and subtly enabled us to become less than we were capable of being. No wonder it is so easy for Nice Women to discount their abilities and accomplishments outside of those associated with the roles of a wife and mother—we often lack the confidence that we ever developed them in the first place.

Our *new voice* speaks a language of respect and support, much like the messages of encouragement that we also identified in Chapter Three. You may recall that many Nice Women had difficulty recalling messages that encouraged them to become independent, self-governing females. These are the messages that recognize our need to grow and to develop our competencies. They are also the messages that encourage us to take educated risks, to solve problems, and to explore options in order to find feasible solutions.

As we takes steps to become more autonomous, we will gain in our feelings of accomplishment. We will learn to respect our own competency and not succumb to old messages that are really putdowns. We need to catch ourselves when we slip into our old habit, and replace the critical messages with ones of self-respect. When we exercise our *new voice* in this way, it becomes a fresh resource for messages that encourage us to grow.

Our New Voice as Director

Throughout much of this book we have discussed the choir of voices or messages in our heads which constantly replay. We have come to the conclusion that while these voices are sometimes nuturing and encouraging, they are too often negative or limiting. It is helpful to visualize our *new voice* as the director of this large vocal choir. If you have ever been part of a choir, you know it is the director's job to coordinate the different sections of the choir so that they sing in harmony and balance.

This is very much the way that our *new voice* works.

In the "critical section" of our personality choir, we have voices that will constantly stir up feelings of shame or inadequacy. These are the voices that see divorce as a black or white issue and will judge us harshly for our "failures." They are also the voices that blame us as divorced or separated women when our children are less than perfect or when we fall short of the "superwoman" expectations that we have of ourselves. These critical voices are extremely destructive to our self-esteem.

It then becomes the job of our *new voice,* or director, to decide who sings, when, where, and for how long. We often need to banish the negative members of our personality choirs; otherwise they will keep us stuck in feelings of guilt and inferiority and prevent the nurturing and encouraging sections of our choir from being heard.

Since it isn't possible to erase all of our limiting or critical messages, our *new voice* is constantly encouraging us to *rethink, reason, and evaluate* our messages in order to achieve harmony. When a critical thought or message is particularly persistent, our *new voice* says, "Okay, I hear you, but you are not in charge here. Go back to your seat, sit down and be quiet!"

At the same time, we may need to encourage our nurturing and encouraging voices to sing louder and stronger. We may need to hold special "practice sessions" in order to strengthen these voices and bring our *new feminine self* into a more balanced state of autonomy. The following exercises represent ways you can hold these "practice sessions" and use them to integrate assertiveness into your *new feminine self.*

In the last chapter of this book, we will examine *selftime* — the final building block of autonomy. We will learn why it is an essential part of our *new feminine self.*

EXERCISES FOR SELF-DISCOVERY

Assessing Our Assertiveness Skills

1. *Asking for What You Need*
Over the next few weeks, tune in to the ways that you ask for what you need. Write these requests or statements down in a small notebook or journal. After considering them, answer the following questions:

Do you continue to use manipulative strategies in asking for what you need?

Do you often accept pat answers that are not satisfying?

Do you feel insecure or stupid to ask again when you don't get answers that you understand?

If you answer "yes" to any of these questions, review the assertive statements on page 167. Using these statements as a model, practice asking for what you need in clear, direct "I" statements. (This may be something as simple as asking for help at the grocery store, or as important as making your child's weekend or holiday visitation arrangements with your ex-spouse.) Make a conscious effort to ask for what you need directly and honestly. Continue to practice these techniques until you integrate them into your *new feminine self.*

2. *Learning to Say "No" without Guilt*
Write down at least four of the requests or situations that are most likely to activate your guilt. These may be requests from your children, your ex-spouse, your ex-in-laws, your family, friends, co-workers, employer, or anyone else who might make a request of you. After thinking them through, answer the following:

What childhood messages are being replayed when I encounter these requests or situations?

How can I modify these messages in order to minimize my guilt? (If you need help, refer to the positive ways to say "no" on page 168.)

3. *Identifying Self-Criticism*
In writing, identify at least three of the ways that you minimize your competencies or put yourself down. Examine them, and then ask yourself:

What childhood message am I replaying?

Then write a replacement statement for each one. The replacement statements should draw upon the messages of encouragement from your *new voice*. (Refer to the list of messages of encouragement in Chapter Three if you need help.)

Practicing these exercises will help your *new voice* become the Director of your personality. As you learn to control those voices that shame, blame, or judge you, your *new voice* will assert your needs with more and more confidence. Also, you will become more generous with yourself when you fall short of your "super woman" expectations.

Ten

Selftime: Making Room
for the New Feminine Self

Selftime, or time set aside to nurture and care for the *new feminine self* we are developing, is the last building block in our journey towards autonomy. For many of us, taking time for ourselves goes directly against our childhood conditioning. While our efforts to take care of the needs of others were reinforced, our efforts to be self-oriented and to take time to care for our own needs were often looked upon as "selfish."

Selftime is a vital part of the process of carving out a *new feminine self*—a self that may want to develop new friendships, take an exercise class, read a good book, plant a garden, or spend the afternoon absorbing the sights, sounds, and smells of a beautiful spring day. As Nice Women, we are notorious for not allowing ourselves the "luxury" of *selftime*. And if we do take some time for ourselves, we feel guilty about all the things we aren't doing while we pursue something that we enjoy. As a result, our efforts are self-defeating. There is a way, however, for us to take time for ourselves and feel good about it.

If we examine the childhood messages that influence our self-defeating behavior, we will most likely discover voices that decry "selfishness" and those that praise us for putting the needs of others before our own. Perhaps we will also detect voices that tell us "all the work should be done before we are allowed to play." My dilemma over attending an exercise class after my son was born is an example of being stuck because of this message. I *wanted* to exercise, but there was always "something" that prevented me from doing it; other tasks took precedence. In reality, however, *I* was the one who would not give myself permission to take the time to get my body back in shape. This is where my *new voice* had to come into play. It was my *new voice* that gave me permission to override my old conditioning.

Our *new voice* directs the nurturing voices in our "personality choir" to become *self*-nurturing. It also gives these self-nurturing voices permission to "practice" so that they may become stronger. As they strengthen, they will become more effective in asserting themselves against the rest of the voices that are continually making demands on our time.

Three Essential Areas of Self-Care

There are three areas of self-care that are essential to the development of our *new feminine self,* and consequently to our autonomy. They are care of the *physical self,* the *social/emotional self,* and the *spiritual self.* If we neglect any of these areas, our lives will lack balance, and there will be gaping holes in the *new feminine self* that we are developing.

Care of our *physical self* means that we are tuned in to our own body and respond to its needs rather than ignore or deny them. This is especially important when we are facing divorce, because our physical energies are easily depleted as our stress level rises. In carving out our *new feminine self,* we need to discover new ways to nuture and replenish our physical self that are both healthy and enjoyable.

One of the most effective ways to do this is through physical activity, or exercise. Of course, this can mean many things—biking, running, dancing, playing sports, walking, climbing mountains, or any activity that allows our body to become invigorated. Most any activity that encourages us to return to a sense of childhood playfulness will benefit us physically as well as emotionally.

There are many studies surrounding the benefits of exercise, particularly vigorous aerobic exercise. Most of these studies conclude that vigorous exercise reduces stress and lowers anxiety. Many of them also support the fact that regular exercise results in increased productivity and in an increased sense of well being. Still another benefit of exercise is that it often diminishes symptoms of depression by utilizing the body's natural mood elevators. Because of its many benefits, exercise can be an effective tool for nurturing ourselves before, during, and after divorce.

After several years, I have finally made regular workouts a part of my life. Four to five times a week I take an exercise class, ride a stationary bike, or climb the stairmaster until the stress of my day has been dissolved by sweat and physical exertion. For me, vigorous exercise has been a crucial factor in combating depression; it helps me feel better about myself both physically and emotionally. To make my exercise more varied and enjoyable, I have learned to rollerblade and have taken up ice skating again. As often as I can, I give the little girl in me who loved to climb trees the opportunity to play through exercise.

Perhaps the most important emotional benefit of physical activity and exercise is the realization that we are reserving *selftime* because we feel we have a self that is worthy of such a commitment. Of course, there will always be many "excuses" which originate in our childhood messages and try to undermine our resolution to make exercise a regular part of our lives. However, through our *new voice,* we can make the choice to increase our physical activity and feel good about it.

Naturally, there are aspects to caring for our physical self other than exercise. Getting enough rest and eating healthy, nutritious foods can also have a positive impact on our *new feminine self.* We must also keep watch over our eating, drinking, smoking, and sleeping habits, since stress can have a negative effect on them and undermine our health as a result. If we feel we are unable to control any of these areas, we may need to seek professional help. Finally, we need to be proactive about all of our female health issues, including regular checkups, breast exams, and pap smears. Both during and after divorce, we need to listen to our body with increased sensitivity and respond to it with the nurturing encouragement of our *new voice.*

Our *social/emotional self* is another aspect of our *new feminine self* that deserves our time and attention. The social/ emotional self integrates how we feel about ourselves, how we perceive others feel about us, and how we respond emotionally to others. It is also that part of us that reacts emotionally to the situations which affect our lives, and at times seem to engulf us. Consequently, our social/emotional self is especially vulnerable during divorce, because virtually no aspect of it is left untouched by the process.

Fortunately, there are a number of healthy strategies for healing and strengthening our social/emotional selves. One of the most effective ways is to stay aware of how we use our childhood coping strategies (as outlined in Chapter Four) and to periodically review the *Exercises For Self-Discovery* on pages 79-82.

When we utilize our *new voice,* we don't deny our feelings. However, we do choose more productive ways to get our needs met. We strive to act—not react. Through exercising our *new voice,* our social/emotional self becomes empowered. The compliant little girl with a long "should" list is no longer in control.

Through the rethinking, reasoning, and evaluating process, the *new feminine self* engages in the behaviors listed below, which are healthier and more productive than our old coping strategies. By doing so, our social/emotional self becomes more resilient and less vulnerable.

new voice	childhood self
expresses feelings	denies/represses feelings
solves problems	feels dependent
asserts needs	sulks or depresses
educates self	feels helpless
tests reality	feels fearful and inadequate

By integrating our *new voice* into our social/emotional self, we are better able to move from the emotionally "stuck" position of the child to the proactive stance of the *new feminine self*.

Another way that we can nurture our social/emotional self is by taking an active role in the management of our depression. Every woman that has contributed to this book has experienced bouts of depression in the process of confronting the numerous issues that surround divorce. Depression can be debilitating, and can require professional help. Even with counseling, however, life goes on, and most of us still have to meet the demands of our day to day lives. Fortunately, there are some things that we can do for ourselves to manage our depression, or at least make it more tolerable.

Depression is "downtime." It is time spent stuck in negative feelings of helplessness, guilt, and loss. It is a kind of mental replay in which we ruminate about our past "failures" and reenact scenarios over which we have no control. No doubt the Nice little girl inside of us is working overtime—still trying to "figure things out" in order to "fix" them.

One of the best ways to combat occurrences of "downtime" is to counteract them with more "uptime." Very simply, this

means we must get up and get going! We can engage in fun
physical activities whenever we can rather than succumb to the
agony of sitting around focusing on how bad we feel. Jenny,
divorced with three young children, illustrates this point well:

> "Weekends were the hardest for me. During the week I
> was working, so I didn't have time to think too much, but
> the weekends seemed to drag on forever. All I did was
> think about how sad and depressed I felt. One weekend
> I had just had enough, so I packed a picnic and put the
> kids in the car. We drove to a large park where there were
> lots of people. We stayed two hours, played wiffle ball
> and frisbee. Then we went to the train museum, climbed
> up in the cars, and rode the trolley around the museum
> grounds. We spent the whole day doing active things.
>
> "Later I noticed that I felt better, less depressed. I
> now plan a special outing every weekend, even if I don't
> *feel* like it. I know that by making a choice to be active,
> I will feel better."

There are many other proactive ways to combat depression.
Actively seeking supportive friendships is an effective one.
There are many of us Nice Women out there who are coping with
similar issues. By forming your own Nice Women support group
you can create a new forum where you can be yourself and share
what you have experienced and what you are feeling with other
women.

Reading books on the subject, or bibliotherapy, as it is often
called, is an another excellent tool in combating depression.
Your local library is an excellent resource for materials on
depression and on a variety of related topics.

When I was experiencing a period of serious depression a
few years ago, I read everything I could find on the subject. I
learned about the different types of depression, what causes it,

and why it affects women so often. I'm sure I read no less than ten books over a two year period, and I did gain a sense of control by educating myself about something that I didn't understand.

There are also excellent books available on improving parenting skills, money management, and finding a new career path. We can gain strength from inspirational books about the lives of women who have triumphed over imposing obstacles or overcome great odds. Reading is a powerful tool because it allows us to take the focus off of ourselves while it empowers us with information at the same time.

Of course, the long-range remedy for chronic depression is to gain control of our lives by staying on a path that will lead to greater autonomy and ultimately a better quality of life. We must keep in mind, however, that the only way to reach our long-term goal is by beginning to take the first steps today.

Because our *spiritual selves* are unique, nurturing our spirituality is a highly individualized experience. It is our spiritual self that asks questions like: "Who am I?" "What is the meaning of life?" "Is there a God?" "Is there an order and purpose to the universe?" "What is my purpose for being on this Earth?" and "How do I achieve peace of mind in such a crazy world?"

The answers to these questions, and spirituality itself, take many shapes and forms. Spirituality is commonly defined as the belief in God or a Higher Power, or that there is a "larger scheme of things" over which we human beings are powerless. For those of us raised in traditional Catholic, Protestant, or Jewish homes, the core of our spiritual self is most likely rooted in our religious training. But no matter what constitutes our sense of spirituality, most of us would agree that it is our spiritual self that seeks peace, inner strength, and solace from a power greater than ourselves.

It is important to the development of our *new feminine self* that we find ways to nourish our spiritual side. Some of us do this by participating in organized religions, some by non-denominational prayer, and some through meditation. Mary Ellen, a mother of two teenagers who was divorced after nineteen years of marriage, shares this experience, which is common to many Nice Women:

> "As a teenager, I pretty much rejected my parent's religion and church in general. I dabbled in various other types of religions in college, but never really returned to attending church as I had done as a child. However, during my divorce and the time since, I have found great comfort in returning to a church very similar to the one I was raised in. It felt very good to reestablish myself in a church, especially where there was support from other single people."

Other women in my workshops have shared their experiences of becoming involved in New Age spiritualism or of joining non-traditional churches that look and feel very different from the traditional ones with which they grew up. Some women talk about developing "inner peace" and "letting go." The important thing is not so much how we develop our spirituality, but that we recognize that we have a spiritual self that needs to be nurtured and attend to that need.

To nurture my own spiritual self, I have learned that I must have some peaceful, spiritual *selftime* in my life. Like most Nice Women, my days and weeks often get very hectic, with the demands of a full-time work schedule and the responsibilities of single parenting to manage. My schedule often leaves little or no time for the peace and quiet that I need to reflect on the good things in my life, count my blessings, and feel grateful. This is when I have to make time for myself. I often do so by making a conscious decision to walk around the lake or to sit in a quiet place for awhile. If I ignore my need to nourish my spiritual self, I sense something is missing from my life.

We all need to take time to nourish our spiritual selves. A good way to start is to explore what our spiritual self meant to us as children and what it means to us now. We can make time to find peace and to reflect on the good things in our lives despite the fact that life is difficult and often presents challenges for which we are not prepared. In doing so we will begin to develop a greater sense of serenity and gratitude.

Making time for ourselves—physically, emotionally, and spiritually—is an important step in our journey towards autonomy. It is essential to the development of our *new feminine self*. Very simply, we cannot feel better about ourselves if we neglect to take care of ourselves.

The following exercises are designed to encourage you to set aside *selftime* for nurturing your physical, social/emotional, and spiritual selves. Like other exercises in this book, keep in mind that real change occurs in small steps that must be practiced over time. By learning positive new behaviors and integrating them into our *new feminine self,* we will increase our self-esteem as well.

EXERCISES FOR SELF-DISCOVERY

Scheduling Selftime

Devote a column on your Commitment Inventory to *selftime*. Decide on specific ways that you want to nurture your physical, social/emotional, and spiritual self. Start with what you can realistically manage. List how many times a week you will do each of these things. List a specific day of the week and time of day, if you feel that will help you stick to your commitment. The activites listed below are suggestions for ways that you can increase your *selftime.*

1. *Physical Activity and Exercise*
Make a commitment to increase your physical activity and to exercise. If you are not currently doing this, start slow with small, manageable steps. Effective exercise can be as simple as a brisk twenty minute walk three or four times a week. Get a friend to walk with you.

Renew an interest in a childhood activity such as rollerskating, biking, or ice skating. Let the little girl within you play through physical activity.

2. *Nurturing Our Social/Emotional Self*
Consciously choose to *rethink, reason, and evaluate* your childhood messages and coping strategies when you begin to feel "stuck." Through your *new voice,* choose more productive behaviors, such as those listed on page 179 in this chapter and page 136 in Chapter Seven.

Take steps to manage your depression by increasing your "uptime." Give yourself permission to play, to pursue new friendships, and to learn new things through reading and attending workshops. Schedule time for these activities on your Commitment Inventory. For example, you could set a goal to read one helpful book each month, or make plans to have lunch with a supportive friend.

3. *Nourishing Your Spiritual Self*
Take a few minutes each day to sit quietly and reflect on your life. Take a mental inventory of the things that you are grateful for. Through your *new voice,* focus on the positive things in your life rather than the negative.

Try to cultivate feelings of peace and serenity in your life. One way to do this is to visualize a scene from your childhood that made you feel especially peaceful. This could be the sun setting over a lake, a sunrise with the dew glistening on the morning grass, or colorful hot air balloons taking off against a clear blue sky.

As you did in the earlier exercise in becoming self-aware, close your eyes, relax your shoulders and concentrate on your breathing. Feel the rhythm of your heartbeat. With your eyes still closed, visualize the peaceful scene from your childhood. See the colors and shapes in your scene. Try to recall the feeling that you had when you originally experienced this scene. Continue to breathe slowly and rhythmically. Try to do this for six to eight minutes each day. Don't be discouraged if this is difficult at first. Like any new skill, it takes time to become comfortable with it.

If you are interested in exploring your spiritual self more fully, you may want to seek out some of the many books and cassette tapes on spiritual development which are available in your local library and bookstore.

Conclusion

I hope now that you have reached the end of this book you will reread it, earmark it, highlight it, and make it your friend and companion, because as I've said so often before, real growth doesn't come easily or quickly. It requires practice and more practice. However, if we make a commitment each day to face the challenges that divorce has placed upon us—physically, emotionally, financially—we will have a better chance of emerging from it as healthier, more autonomous women.

By carefully examining the messages that shaped us, we can takes steps to modify those messages that continue to limit us by reinforcing our helplessness, fear and dependency. This is not easy task. It requires time, energy and a commitment to strengthening our *new feminine self.*

As we progress in our journey toward autonomy, we can benefit from periodically reviewing the *Exercises For Self Discovery* at the end of each chapter of this book, especially when we feel ourselves getting "stuck." We can ask ourselves: "Who or what is making me feel this way? What childhood message am I replaying?" When the message has been identified, it is then possible to move beyond it.

When we have difficulty sorting out what we really *need* to focus on and what we feel we *should* focus on, we can review our "Shoulds" and "Wants" lists in order to regain our perspective. We can also review the childhood coping strategies at the end of Chapter Four to make sure we are not falling back on self-defeating patterns of behavior.

We can design a Commitment Inventory and stick to the goal of becoming financially self-sufficient, or any other important goal we might have. We can make a conscious choice to engage in the proactive behaviors of the *new feminine self,* rather than rely on old ones that do not contribute to growth.

As we grow in our journey toward autonomy—as we *rethink, reason, and evaluate* the messages from our pasts—we will become more integrated. In turn, we will become more aware of what is happening in our lives now and spend less time worrying about our past or our future. We will become more spontaneous and more honest with ourselves and with others.

As we continue to do these things, our *new voice* will get stronger and provide us with messages of respect and encouragement as we struggle to improve our lives. We will discover that in time we will agonize over decisions less and less and begin to feel more and more confident in our ability to make them.

If we practice the skills of self-assertion by utilizing our *new voice,* we will become more effective in getting our needs met in direct, non-manipulative ways. As we take steps to nurture our physical self through increased activity and exercise, we will feel better about our bodies and our emotional selves. By working to actively manage our bouts of depression, we will feel less helpless and more empowered. And by nourishing our spiritual selves, we will enjoy a greater sense of peace in our lives.

No one ever told us that life was going to be easy. Still, most of us never anticipated divorce, and never considered that the resulting conflicts and challenges would be so difficult. We also didn't know that growth and change would be so hard or take so long. However, if we are committed to becoming more autonomous women and to taking steps toward developing our *new feminine self,* it will begin to happen. When it does, we will feel it.

Selected Bibliography

Many books, articles, and life experiences have contributed to the writing of this book. The following list is not intended to be a a complete representation of those resources. Rather, these are books that have been particularly helpful to me during my own journey towards autonomy. They have influenced my writing as well as my work with women. I hope they will be helpful to you as well.

Belenky, Mary F., Clinchy, Blythe M., Goldberger, Nancy R., and Tarule, Jill M., *Women's Ways of Knowing: The Development of Self, Voice, and Mind* (New York: Basic Books, Inc., 1986). Using interviews with women, the authors explore the obstacles women must overcome in developing the power of their minds.

Brenner, Lois and Stein, Robert, *Getting Your Share: A Woman's Guide to Successful Divorce Strategies* (New York: Crown, 1989). Covers legal, tactical, and financial conflicts from a women's perspective.

Bridges, William, *Transitions: Making Sense of Life's Changes* (Reading, Mass.: Addison-Wesley, 1980). Offers a step by step process for coping with life's transitions with an emphasis on beginning anew.

Clarke, Jean Illsley, *Self-Esteem: A Family Affair* (New York: Harper Collins, 1978). Using examples from many different kinds of families, this book outlines effective strategies for promoting self-esteem within families.

De Rosis, Helen, and Pellegrino, Victoria Y, *The Book of Hope: How Women Can Overcome Depression* (New York: Bantam Books, 1976). Helps women understand the causes of depression and offers strategies for overcoming it.

Glasser, William, *Control Theory: A New Explanation of How We Control Our Lives* (New York: Harper and Row, 1985). An important book about regaining control of our lives with an emphasis on creative problem-solving.

Heegaard, Marge, *When Mom and Dad Separate: Children Can Learn to Cope with Grief from Divorce* (Minneapolis: Woodland Press, 1990). An interactive book in which children ages 6-12 are encouraged to draw and write about their feelings about divorce.

Jack, Dana C, *Silencing the Self: Women and Depression* (Cambridge, Mass.: Harvard University Press, 1991). Explores the origin of female depression with an emphasis on early patterns of compliance.

James, Muriel and Jongeward, Dorothy, *Born to Win: Transactional Analysis with Gestalt Experiments* (Reading, Mass.: Addison-Wesley, 1971). Shows the reader useful ways to discover the many parts of her personality, to integrate them, and to develop a core of self-confidence.

Jongeward, Dorothy and Scott, Dru, *Women As Winners: A Guide to Understanding, Growth, and Authenticity* (Reading, Mass.: Addison-Wesley, 1976). Examines the socialization of females; includes exercises to help women increase their awareness and fulfill their potential.

Krementz, Jill, *How It Feels When Parents Divorce* (New York: Alfred A. Knopf, 1984). Nineteen children, ages eight to sixteen, share their stories about their parents' divorces.

Lansky, Vicki, *Divorce Book for Parents: Helping Your Children Cope With Divorce and Its Aftermath* (New York: New American Library, 1989). A practical guide for parents and children coping with the challenges presented by divorce.

Peck, M. Scott, *The Road Less Traveled: A New Psychology of Love, Traditional Values, and Spiritual Growth* (New York: Simon and Schuster, 1978). An enlightening look at the painful process of confronting and solving life's problems, with an emphasis on spiritual growth.

Sanford, Linda T., and Donovan, Mary E, *Women & Self-Esteem: Understanding and Improving the Way We Think and Feel About Ourselves* (New York: Anchor/Doubleday, 1984). An overview of women's self-esteem problems, with remedial exercises.

Schaef, Anne Wilson, *Co-Dependence: Misunderstood—Mistreated* (San Francisco: Harper and Row, 1986). Expands the common definition of co-dependence to include the highly socialized woman.

Viorst, Judith, *Necessary Losses: The Loves, Ilusions, Dependencies, and Impossible Expectations That All of Us Have to Give Up in Order to Grow.* (New York: Simon and Schuster, 1986). A well researched book that examines the nature of life's losses as well as their inevitability.

Geneva Sugarbaker, M.S. is the Director of *Workshops for Women,* which counsels women in transition on personal, educational, and career issues. She has published in professional journals on the subjects of self-esteem, career development, and females and underachievement. A single parent of a son and daughter, she lives in Minneapolis.